PHONOGRAPH
DOLLS AND TOYS
BY
JOAN & ROBIN ROLFS

DEDICATION

To our Family. To Joan's parents, Esther and Louis Zeeman, who placed a Victrola in Joan's bedroom when she was a child of two, to be played and enjoyed. Joan's brother, Bruce Zeeman, who broke the Victrola and sparked Robin's interest in the restoration and technology of the phonograph. Our niece, Becky who loves to play with phonograph dolls and to our nephews, Patrick, Dan, William and Ben who enjoy phonograph toys.

First Edition

First Printing 2004
Copyright 2004 Joan & Robin Rolfs
Authors may be contacted at: www.audioantique.com

ISBN#: 0-9606466-6-3

Published by Mulholland Press, Inc.
14332 Mulholland Drive
Los Angeles, CA 90077

Also available from Mulholland Press:

Look for the Dog, An Illustrated Guide to Victor Talking Machines
Columbia Phonograph Companion, Volume I
Edison Cylinder Phonograph Companion
Edison Disc Phonographs and Diamond Discs
Edison Blue Amberol Recordings, 1912-1914
Edison Blue Amberol Recordings, 1915-1929
The Victor Data Book

For the latest list of publications, visit:

www.mulhollandpress.com

CONTENTS

PRICE GUIDE

This price guide is basically as it states. It is only a guide for the value of the phonograph dolls, toys, gramophones, and children's records found in this book. A range of prices exist for any one item. Price will vary due to a variety of criteria, including (but not limited to) the: rarity of the item, popularity of the item, locality in which the item is being bought or sold and most importantly condition. Original dresses will increase the value of a doll, original boxes will add to the value of toy phonographs and toys. Original sleeves will add to the value of children's records. But most significant is the condition of the children's toy. Most children loved their dolls and toys and the fact that the condition of many of those that have survived show signs of wear and are in a well used condition is a tribute to the inventor's success in creating a well designed product. Many toys of our childhood have an intrinsic or sentimental value and wax nostalgic memories which may greatly exaggerate the value of the piece beyond expectations. Whatever the factors affecting price, it is the joy of collecting and preserving artifacts of the past that bring the buyer and seller together to mutually benefit the hobby.

Values are denoted in the captions of the item and rated by a letter value.
Below is the rating code for items:

A	$12000 and up
B	$7000 - $11999
C	$3000 - $6999
D	$1500 - $2999
E	$750 - $1499
F	$300 - $749
G	$100 - $299
H	$50 - $99
I	Under $50

ACKNOWLEDGMENTS

Phonograph Dolls that Talk and Sing was a book we co-authored with Bessie and Floyd Seiter. We had a great deal in common with Bessie and Floyd. We were instructors, enjoyed collecting phonographs and both Joan and Bessie loved to collect phonograph dolls. It was a pleasure to complete the unpublished draft of a doll book that Bessie and Floyd dreamed of publishing. The book sold very well and we gathered more information on phonograph dolls from collectors, doll lovers and doll manufacturers. We discussed the doll book with our phonograph friends. Don Gfell (our Mr. Edison) had the bright idea of expanding the concept of the book to include phonograph toys. We embraced the idea and you are now reading the introduction to a book on phonograph dolls, children's phonographs, phonograph toys and records that were made to entertain and enchant children of all ages.

We want to thank all the collectors, friends and historians who shared their knowledge, collections and expertise:
Jean-Paul Agnard, Teri A. Andolina, Julien Anton, Edward Ardolino, Paul Baker, Lynn Bilton, Lyle Boehland, Bill Chambers, Dan Choffnes, Bob & Wendie Coon, Aaron & Thea Cramer, Larry & Sandy Crandell, Deanna Danner, Domenic DiBernardo, Tim Fabrizio, Patrick Feaster, Joyce Gearhart, Bert & Evelyn Gowans, John & Garnet Hauger, Joe Hilton, Charlie Hummel, Don & Bobbie Gfell, Charles Gregory, Howard Hazelcorn, Nina & Dave Heitz, Larry Hudson, Warren Kelm, Ron & Janet Keuler, William E. Klinger, Allen Koenigsberg, Neil & Carole Maken, Scott Malawski, Carole & John Mehling, Peter Muldavin, Joan Mulligan, Diane & Kurt Nauck, Shawn & Beth O'Rourke, George Paul, Ray Phillips, Mary Virginia Pollard, Pluethipol Prachumphol, Stephan Puille, Steve Ramm, Barbara & Joseph Regan, Rene Rondeau, Lawrence A. Schlick, Anthony & Donna Sinclair, Karyn Sitter, Merle Sprinzen, Roxanne Wallis, Charlie Weatherbee, Frances & John Wiedey, James R. Wilkins, Jeff & Tonya Young, Dick & Jean Zahn, and the Zeeman family. A special thank you to Floyd Seiter for his support and encouragement.

We also appreciate the research and photographs provided by: Laurence J. Russell, Edison Birthplace Association Inc., Milan Ohio; Edison-Ford Estates, Fort Meyers Florida and The City of London Phonograph and Gramophone Society Ltd.

A final note of appreciation to Robert Baumbach, our publisher, for his patience, insight and professionalism.

INTRODUCTION

It all began on July 18th, 1877 when Thomas A. Edison spoke a nursery rhyme, "Mary had a little Lamb" into the mouthpiece of a great new invention he called the phonograph. Success at reproducing recorded sound inspired subsequent patented improvements eventually leading to the commercial success of the phonograph. Strangely, the perfection of the phonograph had beginnings in the development of a talking doll for children. Though not commercially successful, the development of the beautiful Edison doll that talked did generate the first commercial recordings for the public. From a spoken nursery rhyme to a symphony orchestra, recorded sound has brought delight and enjoyment to millions. Entertainment for children was one of the first purposes of the phonograph, and talking dolls, toys, children's phonographs and records have been marketed for children ever since.

Many books and resources are available on phonographs and records; however, there are few sources for phonograph toys, dolls and records for children. This book will place emphasis on historical dolls and toys that have technical developments that influenced the industry. We were always drawn to these fun antiques of the past that were treasured by children. They had to be treasured or they would not survive for our enjoyment today. Although this book will not cover every child's phonograph, doll, toy or record, we hope it will give you the knowledge and appreciation of these wondrous playthings for children of the Victorian age to the computer age.

CHAPTER 1

EARLY PHONOGRAPH DOLLS AND TOYS

The attempt to mimic the human voice by mechanical means is a formidable task. To artificially duplicate the organs of the mouth, lips, tongue, larynx and lungs to replicate human speech involved materials and technology that were largely beyond the scope of early nineteenth century doll makers. Of course, this did not discourage attempts by doll makers to incorporate ingenious devices that made childlike sounds by means of bellows, reeds, resonators, whistles and organ pipes. Complex air powered speech synthesizers were incorporated into automatons and larger clockwork mechanisms that were exhibited to the delight and fascination of the public.

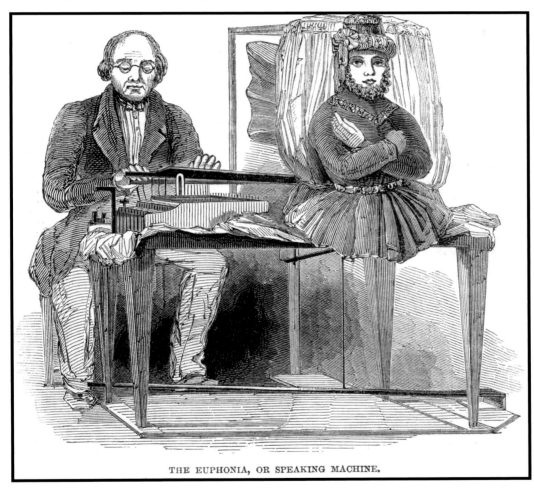

THE EUPHONIA, OR SPEAKING MACHINE.

The Euphonia, or Speaking Machine Engraving. Patrick Feaster Collection.

One of the first successful attempts at producing artificial speech by mechanical means was demonstrated in the late eighteenth century by the Hungarian, Wolfgang von Kempelen (1734 - 1804). His machine consisted of bellows, reeds, whistles and a resonant cavity, which were manipulated by the hands of the operator to simulate vowel sounds and words that could be combined to form short sentences. Later, the English scientist Charles Wheatstone, while appointed professor of experimental physics at King's College, London, demonstrated a similar device to produce speech sounds. Previously, Wheatstone demonstrated his skill in acoustic research as an accomplished musician and instrument maker.

Perhaps the most successful innovation in the field of speech synthesis was presented around 1840 by Joseph Faber. Schooled as a mathematician with an interest in music, he became obsessed with developing a talking machine. In a complex machine, which he dubbed the "Euphonia," bellows operated by a foot pedal forced air through a complex chamber that incorporated a model of the tongue, lips and pharyngeal cavity. Activated by a keyboard of sixteen keys, the skilled operator could control the air flow and shape of the cavity in a way to produce vocal sounds. Reportedly the work of twenty-five years of labor, it could produce whispered speech, ordinary speech in several languages and even sing "God Save the Queen." For exhibition purposes, the machine was housed in the torso of an automaton with moving eyes and lips.

In terms of producing a talking doll for the purpose of being a child's toy, there was very little that could be applied in the way of the aforementioned scientific instruments of artificial speech. Aside from the cost and fabrication necessary to miniaturize the components to the size necessary for a doll, the concept of operating all these devices relied on a skilled person to form the parts of speech one element at a time and flow them together to produce the likeness of speech. This was a task beyond the average parent, let alone a child.

Dolls equipped with small bellows and reed mechanisms did provide children with sounds of "Ma ma," "Pa pa," baby crying and sounds to entertain the imagination of delighted children. Perhaps one of the more entertaining of these dolls was the Webber Singing Doll produced by William Augustus Webber and distributed by the Massachusetts Organ Co. from 1882 - 1885. Although it was incapable of speech it did "sing" by means of a small bellows and reed organ placed in the body of the doll. The instrument incorporated a raceway that automatically advanced a sheet of perforated paper containing one of 27 tunes available. By pressing the front of the doll body, the child could activate the mechanism. The doll had a wax head with real hair, soft cloth body and leather arms. It was available in three sizes and price points: No. 1 was 22 inches in length priced at $2.75. No. 2 was 24 inches at $3.25. No 3 was 26 inches at $4.00. Each had a larger "singing attachment" and the largest had a bigger head and sleep eyes. Clothes were extra! A simple embroidered chemise was 25 cents extra while undergarments and costume with lace trim ranged from $3.00 to $5.00. All this added up to a great deal of money for the top of the line model. (Don't forget the additional music cards.) The unreliable mechanism that often jammed or broke led to many disappointed children, frustrated parents and very poor sales.

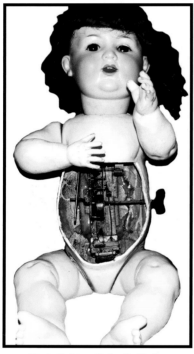

Early Talking Doll with Bellows.
Anthony & Donna Sinclair Collection.
(Value F)

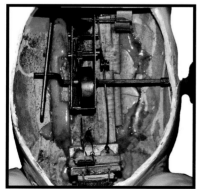

Bellows Found Inside
Early Talking Doll.

Webber Singing Doll Ad. *Harpers Weekly* 1882.
Neil & Carole Maken Collection. (Value I)

Until a simple method of storing and reproducing speech could be devised, children of the day would have to be content with dolls and stuffed toys incorporating simple reed and bellows mechanisms that could produce sounds resembling "Ma ma," a baby's cry, the bleating of a lamb or the "moo" of a cow. It was no wonder then that the invention of a device that could actually record and play back the human voice was met with great wonder and amazement. At first, met with skepticism and disbelief when demonstrated before members of the *Scientific American,* the phonograph was the wonder of the age. So astonishing was the result that observers concluded that trickery or hidden components must have been incorporated in the demonstration. The inventor himself insisted that a child could operate it and its principle of operation was quite simple to understand. It wasn't long before the phonograph became an immediate hit with the scientific community and curious public. Strangely, Thomas Alva Edison's invention of the phonograph in 1877 was more the result of experiments in electricity, the telephone, telegraphy and acoustic research rather than the mechanics of synthetic speech. Knowledge based upon the electromechanics of the telephone and the repeating or embossing telegraph provided the impetus for this remarkable invention. Yet the working model did not contain any electrical components. In fact its mechanical simplicity of operation and lack of electrical mystery contributed to skepticism regarding the authenticity of the invention.

The inventor's original intention for "his baby," the phonograph, was for scientific, business and educational purposes. "The main utility of the phonograph, however, being for the purpose of letter writing and other forms of dictation..." He was reluctant to see his invention used for commercial entertainment purposes. Edison insisted that it was not meant to be used as a toy for pure amusement. Of course, the public thought differently and was intrigued by the novelty of the machine to record and play back a cornet solo of *Yankee Doodle* or the voice of a stage actor reciting a humorous monologue.

Machines were made available for lease whereby enterprising promoters of stage shows would fill large entertainment halls with people eager to hear the machine sing in a foreign language, a slow ballad played back rapidly at a high pitch, the barking of dogs and other clever maneuvers to demonstrate the remarkable abilities of the invention.

THE PHONOGRAPH AND ITS INVENTOR, MR. THOMAS A. EDISON.

It is somewhat ironic that the first commercial recordings to be made available to the public were not for utilitarian business purposes, but would be children's nursery rhymes to be sold with a $10.00 doll.

Child's Blocks.
Bob & Wendie Coon Collection. (Value I)

EDISON TALKING DOLL

It was the genius of a wizard that made dolls talk. Thomas A. Edison known as the "Wizard of Menlo Park" invented the phonograph in 1877. The first words he spoke into the "Tinfoil Phonograph" was a nursery rhyme: "Mary Had A Little Lamb." After the invention of the phonograph in 1877, Thomas A. Edison expressed the idea that he would like to invent a talking doll and other toys that would produce sounds for children. A company was formed called The Edison Toy Manufacturing Company. Actually Edison didn't do much work on the doll. The two main workers on the project were William W. Jacques and Charles Batchelor. In fact it was William W. Jacques who first developed a prototype based on Edison's original tinfoil phonograph. Jacques and his partner Lowell Briggs founded the Edison Phonograph Toy Manufacturing Company of Maine in 1887, with Edison agreeing to lend his name to the planned product in return for royalties and stock ownership. It was in 1878 that Thomas A. Edison obtained a British patent for a "phonographic" doll that would reproduce sound.

Madeleine Edison Sloane, Daughter of Thomas A. Edison, With Her Edison Doll. The Edison Birthplace Association, Inc. Collection, Milan Ohio.

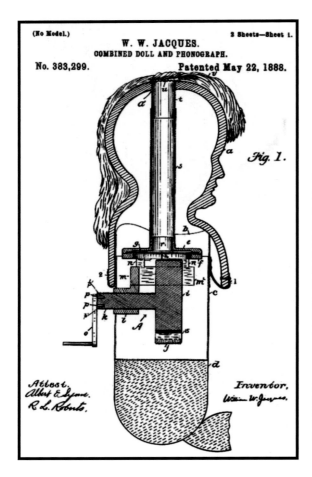

The first Edison talking doll did not look much like the doll he manufactured in 1890. The Jacques patent drawing shows a doll with a stuffed body and shoulder head with the sound funnel coming up into the head. He obtained two British patents, a U.S., and a French patent for phonograph dolls with the record playing device inside the body of the doll. It was operated by turning a key or small crank. Before production began, Edison took over the company in 1890 and the doll was placed on the market. The Edison doll had been twelve years in the making. There were fourteen patents from 1878 through 1890, a lot of lost money and many hard feelings.

HARPER'S YOUNG PEOPLE, January 27, 1891, described the first doll with a tin cylindrical housing about six inches long to hold the phonograph. A funnel at the upper end of this tin cylindrical housing is where the sound was to come forth. It was a crude doll that looked more like a stovepipe with arms and legs than a beautiful talking doll.

In October of 1887, William W. Jacques of Newton, Mass. patented a doll with a record playing device within its body. He assigned the rights to the Edison Phonograph Toy Manufacturing Co. of Maine. On July 2, 1889, Edison filed an application for a "Phonograph Doll and Other Toys." Interestingly, this application specified the use of:

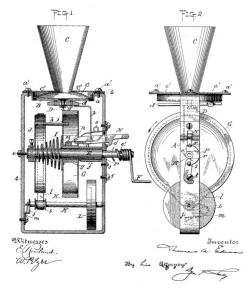

(No Model.)

T. A. EDISON.
PHONOGRAPH FOR DOLLS OR OTHER TOYS.
No. 423,039.   Patented Mar. 11, 1890.

"A stationary reproducer with a screw thread on the cylinder sleeve advancing the cylinder on the shaft." "A sound record made in a hard wax-like composition." "The reproducing-point is preferably a ball." "The ring (record) is removable from the drum it being held on simply by friction......so that when the sound-record is worn out......the rings may be changed by the user and thus a variety of reproduced matter be secured."

The April 26, 1890, issue of the *SCIENTIFIC AMERICAN* magazine contained a very interesting article about Thomas Edison's latest invention, the phonograph doll. The article described in full the extent of the production of the doll in Edison's plant. It claimed that 500 dolls could be produced in one day, and that one half of the plant was devoted to the manufacture of the doll.

Photo of Edison Doll Manufacturing. Edison National Site. U.S. Department of Interior Collection.

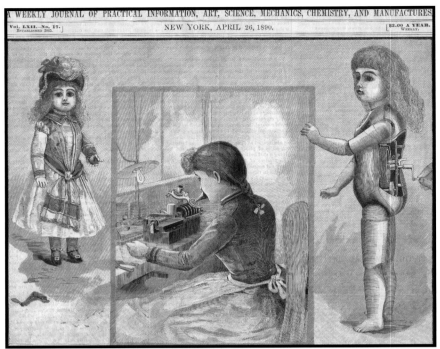

A WEEKLY JOURNAL OF PRACTICAL INFORMATION, ART, SCIENCE, MECHANICS, CHEMISTRY, AND MANUFACTURES

Vol. LXII.—No. 17.
Established 1845.   NEW YORK, APRIL 26, 1890.   [$3.00 A YEAR.
WEEKLY.

Much of the mechanism of the doll was produced in the regular phonograph making area, while the wax cylinders were made in a separate part of the plant. The cylinders were placed on a machine similar to a phonograph and a young woman spoke the message that was recorded on the wax cylinder. Since there were about eighteen women talking at the same time in small booths, the area became very noisy. The name of one of the young voices is known: Julia Miller, daughter of Walter Miller, an Edison employee.

The doll could be purchased with a simple or elaborate dress. The Edison doll with a simple chemise sold for $10.00. The simple chemise was an off white dress with bands of ribbon trim. A silk tie was found around the waistline. Smocking and ribbon trim highlighted the neckline. These dresses were also trimmed with colored ribbon and made of various colors of lightweight cotton batiste fabric. The elaborate dress was a Victorian style. Intricate embroidered decorations were found on the collar, sleeves and front of the dress. The dress was highlighted with a beautiful sash at the waist. The hat had a wide brim with a feather plume. The elaborately dressed Edison doll sold for $20.00 to $25.00.

Edison Doll, Original Chemise Dress. Edison Birthplace Association, Inc., Milan Ohio. (Value A)

Edison Doll, Elaborate Replica Dress. Neil & Carole Maken Collection. (Value A)

Edison Doll Head Marked S & H 719.

Edison Doll Showing Jointed Wood Limbs and Tin Body With Holes in the Chest.
Simon and Halbig Head. No Motor. (Value C)

The Edison doll featured a bisque head made by either Simon and Halbig or Bahr and Proschild. The Bahr and Proschild doll is marked "224" Size 12. The Simon and Halbig dolls are marked with various marks that are "S & H 719," "S12H 719" or "SH 719-12." Both were German companies. A few dolls have been found with Jumeau heads, but these were probably replacements. She has a long human hair wig, pierced ears and expressive paperweight eyes. Eye and hair color vary on the Edison Dolls. The hands and feet were made of wood, a common practice in those days. The Edison doll can be found with hands that are rigid or movable at the wrists. The doll was 22 inches tall, however she did vary slightly in length. The doll weighed four pounds. Bodies of the Edison doll were made from tinplate pieces. Presses were used in the forty-five operations that stamped and cut out six heavy metal pieces that formed the body and held the phonograph mechanism. Some early Edison dolls were also known to have painted bodies. A majority of the dolls had the unpainted tin body. The Edison doll was not necessarily cuddly; instead she was a mechanical marvel of the great inventor, Thomas A. Edison. She was to be treasured rather than hugged. She was the incredible talking doll of the 19th century.

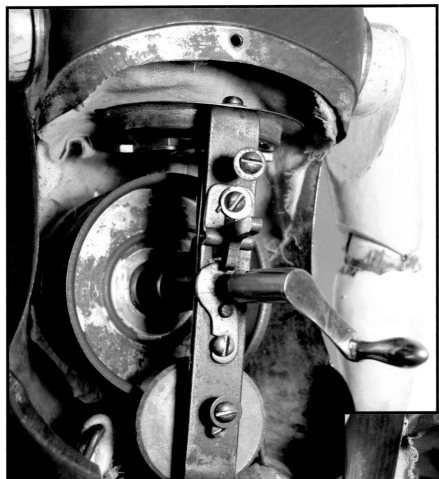

The body was made with two pieces of tin fastened together with screws. Some of the metal bodies have a list of patent dates stamped on the back of the dolls' bodies and some have no markings. The holes in the upper chest also vary in design. Some dolls have a round pattern of holes. Other Edison dolls have the holes spreading across the chest to let the sound come forth. The phonograph mechanism fits tightly inside the body with a crank protruding out of the back of the doll. There was no spring and the crank had to be turned constantly and very evenly to produce sound.

Edison Doll Mechanism. Julien Anton Collection.

The 1890 patent specified a ball reproducing stylus and a mechanical device that disengaged the stylus at the end of play and returned the record to the starting position. Although Edison's patent caveat stated that a sapphire stylus could be employed, the production doll employed a metal stylus, a decision that would later haunt the inventor. The record and motor are rarely found intact. A reproduction motor and cylinder can be purchased and installed to bring the Edison doll back to its original condition. Of course there is nothing that will replace the original motor and cylinder, which adds to the rarity of the doll.

Reproducer and Return Mechanism.

Edison Motor Paper Label. Julien Anton Collection. (Value E)

Today collectors covet the Edison doll with or without the original motor. Only about a dozen are known to survive with the motor intact. Many more of these dolls with mechanisms may exist in private collections. Most of the surviving phonograph mechanisms have a paper label with printed patent information pasted to the small horn. A few are also known to have this information stamped on the metal of the horn. Most do not have the cylinder record intact, as they were broken in shipment or from use. This motor was an ingenious design, but not practical for a child's toy.

Replica mechanisms have been made throughout the years. In the 1960s Elmer Jones, a well-known phonograph collector, produced about a dozen motors. Neil Maken also made a small number for the centennial of the Edison doll in 1990, which had a sapphire stylus. Steve Walker also made 15 replicas in 1990. Darren Wallace of Canada made the most precise copies in 2001. They are extremely precise in every detail including aged metal parts. The reproduction motors can be installed within the body of the doll to bring it back to the original condition.

Original Doll Mechanism, Stamped Label.
Rene Rondeau Collection. (Value E)

Reproduction Doll Mechanism Made by
Darren Wallace, Canada 2001. (Value E)

The Edison doll was not a user friendly item. The doll cylinder was a fragile wax ring, three inches in diameter and a half-inch wide. Charles Batchelor's model of the Edison doll of 1888 used a wax or metallic soap cylinder. The cylinder was very delicate and was easily broken. The record would play for 15 to 20 seconds. The crank or key could be removed from the back of the doll and easily lost. If a cylinder broke, the owner could not replace the cylinder without completely taking the doll apart. There was a feed screw, but no spring motor nor a mechanical governor. The steel stylus tore up the wax cylinder and did not withstand a child's abuse. The cylinder of the phonograph is mounted on a sleeve that slides on the shaft. The sleeve is threaded, causing the cylinder to travel laterally under the fixed reproducer. The cylinder advanced at a pitch of 56 threads per inch. As the child turned the crank to play a song, a small flywheel helped maintain speed. When a release lever above the crank was pressed, the stylus was raised and the cylinder returned to the start of play position.

Reproduction Wax Cylinder Made by Jean-Paul Agnard of Musee Edison Du Phonographe in Quebec Canada 1998. The Recording on the Cylinder is "Mary Had A Little Lamb" Recorded by Claire Fabrizio. (Value G)

The dolls were purchased by the name of the nursery rhyme they contained. They came with an instruction card with directions for winding. The card stated: "Place handle on shaft and wind by turning to the right, keeping count 1, 2, 3, 4. The doll will talk slow or fast, and the regular time can be easily acquired by a little practice. After it has ceased talking, pull down the back spring and it is ready to talk again."

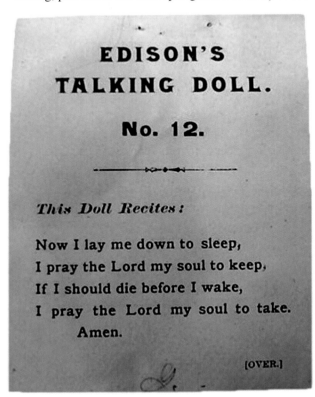

EDISON'S
TALKING DOLL.

No. 12.

This Doll Recites:

Now I lay me down to sleep,
I pray the Lord my soul to keep,
If I should die before I wake,
I pray the Lord my soul to take.
Amen.

[OVER.]

Original Edison Doll Song Title Card.
Nina and Dave Heitz Collection. (Value G)

There were twelve nursery rhymes as follows:

1. *Mary Had a Little Lamb.*
2. *Twinkle, Twinkle Little Star.*
3. *There Was a Little Girl and She Had a Little Curl.*
4. *Little Bo-Peep.*
5. *Little Tom Tucker.*
6. *Hiccory, Diccory, Dock.*
7. *Little Jack Horner.*
8. *Ba-Ba, Black Sheep.*
9. *Jack and Jill.*
10. *Two Little Black Birds.*
11. *Old Mother Hubbard.*
12. *Now I Lay Me Down to Sleep.*

Edison Doll Stand. Robin & Joan Rolfs Collection.
(Value D)

Base of Edison Doll Stand.

Ten thousand Edison dolls were put together in the U.S. with only 2500 approved for shipment. The dolls were first sold to the public at the Edison exhibit in the NYC Lenox Lyceum on April 7, 1890. The Edison phonograph doll was marketed as "The Greatest Wonder of the Age." The doll may have been displayed on a custom made stand. A brass plated cast iron base with raised letters proclaimed "Edison's Talking Doll." The rope designed upright support could be adjusted to accommodate the doll. The stand is very rare. Its origin is not known, but it may be from the NYC Lyceum or an early department store display.

Edison Doll with Motor.
Elaborate Replica Dress.
Rene Rondeau Collection. (Value A)

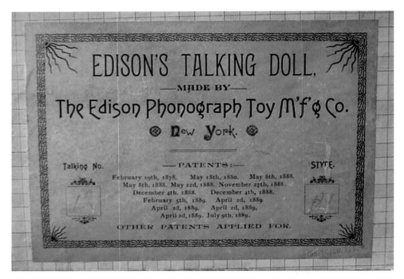

EDISON'S TALKING DOLL,
— MADE BY —
The Edison Phonograph Toy M'f'g Co.
⊛ New York. ⊛

Talking No.   STYLE.

— PATENTS: —

February 19th, 1878.   May 18th, 1880.   May 8th, 1888.
May 8th, 1888. May 22d, 1888. November 27th, 1888.
December 4th, 1888.   December 4th, 1888.
February 5th, 1889.   April 2d, 1889.
April 2d, 1889.   April 2d, 1889.
April 2d, 1889. July 9th, 1889.

OTHER PATENTS APPLIED FOR.

Original Edison Doll With Motor in Box.
Nina & Dave Heitz Collection. (Value A)

The doll was boxed in an attractive cardboard plaid box. The label affixed to the end of the box stated the patent dates. A handwritten number on the label denoted the doll cylinder placed on the Edison doll. The labels on the boxes vary with two different labels. Later dolls sold without the phonograph mechanism had a completely different label pasted on top of the original Edison label.

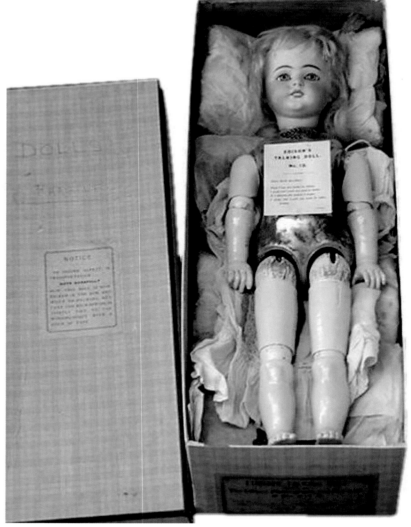

This talking doll was not the success that Edison had originally envisioned. Complaints from companies were reaching the Edison Toy Company. A letter received April 24, 1890 from San Francisco said that among twenty dolls received, two were broken, four wouldn't talk, and because of the high freight, the writer said he couldn't afford to sell the dolls at New York prices. By late April of 1890, dolls were withdrawn from sale. Some had loose works, some would not talk, and after an hour of playing some were so faint they could not be heard. In addition, there was the complaint that the cost of the doll and the cost to return it were excessive. Edison's talking doll experiment was a costly experience. "The voices of the little monsters were exceedingly unpleasant to hear" he later remarked. In November 1895 an agreement was reached between Edison and the Toy Company that manufactured the dolls, which stipulated that all the dolls in storage, both complete and incomplete, would revert to the Toy Company for liquidation. Many remaining dolls were sold without phonograph works. All told, less than 500 dolls were ever sold with the phonograph complete. A large part of the unsold inventory was shoveled under the earth at West Orange, N.J. where the doll burial ground remains to this day. Despite its fragility the doll was not a complete failure. It contained the first automatic record-playing device, and contained the first pre-recorded records to be sold under the name "Edison." The Edison Doll made three important contributions to the phonograph industry according to the late George L. Frow in his book *Edison Cylinder Phonograph Companion*.

They were:

1) The doll contained the first automatic record playing mechanism.
2) The first phonograph records sold to the public under the name Edison were made for the Talking Doll.
3) The doll had pre-recorded cylinders, hence in February 1889 they were the first entertainment cylinders.

Original Edison Phonograph Toy Stock Certificate. Charlie Hummel Collection. (Value C)

KAMMER & REINHARDT DOLL

The Kammer & Reinhardt doll introduced circa 1890 had a significant impact on the technology of recorded sound well into the 20th century. Emile Berliner, who emigrated from Germany in 1870, developed a method for producing a flat disc recording and a mechanism for playing back the recording on a device he termed a Gramophone. This was the first flat record using a lateral method to record and play records rather than the hill-and-dale (vertical) method of cylinder recording produced by Thomas A. Edison. It was as early as 1889, according to some sources, that the well-known German doll manufacturer

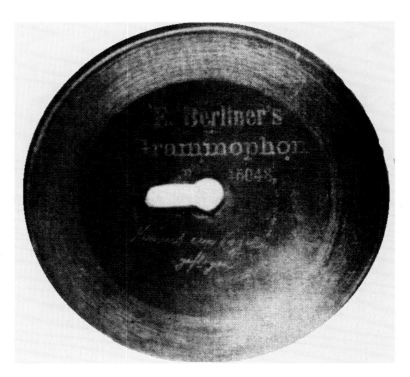

Crude Drawing of Doll Showing Gramophone in Position.

Kammer & Reinhardt Puppenfabrik. (Circa 1885)

Kammer & Reinhardt approached Emile Berliner to develop a device to make their dolls talk. Another likelihood is that Kammer & Reinhardt met Emile Berliner during the Leipzig fair of 1890 when he was looking for investors in Germany. It was a crude mechanism and sold more as a novelty than a doll to be played with by children. This doll is exceedingly rare with only one partial example known to exist in a museum in Germany. Kammer & Reinhardt was one of the leading German doll companies from 1885-1932. The company was based in Waltershausen, Germany. Ernst Kammer, a sculptor, and Franz Reinhardt, a merchant were the founders. They often used bisque heads made by Simon and Halbig on their dolls. The firm exhibited and won prizes at the World's Columbian Exposition in Chicago in 1893 and the St. Louis World's Fair in 1904.

The small mechanism in the interior of the doll's body was set in motion by a hand crank. The reproducer automatically came down upon the small disc and a song was played. Above the hand crank there was a handle that put the reproducer back into the starting position by a counterclockwise rotation.

The disc records were interchangeable and could be played repeatedly. It should be noted that the songs were recorded in German. The doll used an 8 cm. (3 1/8 inch) diameter record. The spindle hole of the tiny disc was key-shaped and kept it from slipping. One of the little discs played *Kommt ein Vogerl geflogen*, an old German folk song. This 3 1/8 inch size disc was used solely for the phonograph dolls. The patent number was immediately above the "keyhole" of the record. A label glued to the back of the record contained the lyrics of the song. The pressing materials of the records were either celluloid or hard rubber. The Kammer & Reinhardt Company was experienced in the use of both materials, although the companies of GFKC and Rhenische Gummi und Celluloid Fabrik Werkes of Neckerau, Germany are also credited for the pressings.

Berliner Record Used in the Kammer & Reinhardt Doll. (Value C)

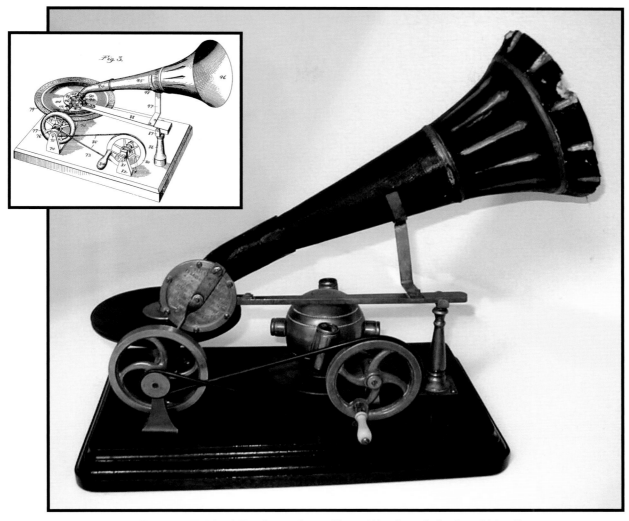

Kammer & Reinhardt Toy Gramophone. Howard Hazelcorn Collection. (Value A)

KAMMER & REINHARDT TOY GRAMOPHONE

Toy Gramophones were produced by the toy firm of Kammer & Reinhardt of Germany under the patent of Emile Berliner from 1890 to 1894. These machines sold in Europe and Britain, but few ever made it to the States. Berliner's main interest at this time was to produce an economical alternative to the cylinder record. The simplicity of construction was cost effective. Though simple in operation, its performance relegated it to the category of a child's toy. The earliest model of this Kammer & Reinhardt Toy Gramophone had a decorated cast iron base. The paper mache horn was self-supporting and the machine was hand driven.

The 1891 Kammer & Reinhardt Toy Gramophone had a wood base with a decorative paper mache horn. The sphere shown in the above photo is for attaching listening tubes. Kammer & Reinhardt also produced 5 inch records that were not for the doll between 1890 and 1893 in pressing plants in Germany and possibly in France and the UK. It is uncertain how many different records (individually numbered) with German, English, French and other music and talking exist, but there are hundreds for certain. No evidence has shown that Emile Berliner recorded his own voice, as he was not directly involved in the project (aside from licensing Kammer & Reinhardt) and was only in Germany a very short time.

Early Kammer & Reinhardt Toy Gramophone.
Domenic DiBernardo Collection. (Value A)

Columbia Toy Graphophone with Original Box.   Shawn & Beth O'Rourke Collection. (Value A)

Columbia Toy Record and Box.
Shawn & Beth O'Rourke Collection. (Value E)

COLUMBIA TOY GRAPHOPHONE

Anxious to enter the Gramophone market but hampered by production delays of a quality machine, Columbia introduced the Toy Graphophone for the 1899 Christmas trade. This small Columbia could easily fit in the palm of your hand. It was introduced at the cost of $3.00 and came with five records for children. Records with adult content could be purchased separately. The 3 3/8 inch brown wax records were vertically cut and inside start. The Columbia Toy, horn and reproducer were included in a wooden box with directions for operation printed on the outside of the box. There are two known versions of this box. One has more colorful graphics than the version shown. Despite its diminutive entry, the Toy Graphophone does represent the first disc phonograph to be offered to the public by an American manufacturer. Although low in cost, sales of the Toy were very limited.

Toy Gramophone Dec. 1900. Lawrence A. Schlick Collection. (Value A)

TOY GRAMOPHONE

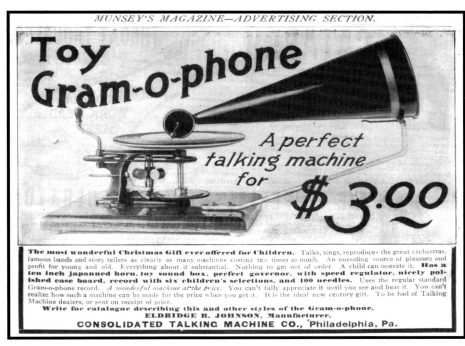

Original Ad for Toy Gram-O-Phone. (Value I)

Emile Berliner became successful in Germany, but to broaden his market and to get out of the toy category he needed a motor driven disc player. The search for a motor led him to Camden, New Jersey and a machinist by the name of Eldridge Johnson. Eldridge Johnson was successful in developing a spring motor for the Gramophone and by 1896 had a contract to manufacture the entire machine. By December of 1900 the Toy Gramophone manufactured by Eldridge R. Johnson entered the market. The ad stated: "Toy Gram-O-Phone. A perfect talking machine for $3.00. The most wonderful Christmas Gift ever offered for children. A child can operate it. Has a ten inch japanned horn, toy sound box, perfect governor, with speed regulator, nicely polished case board, record with six children's selections, and 100 needles."

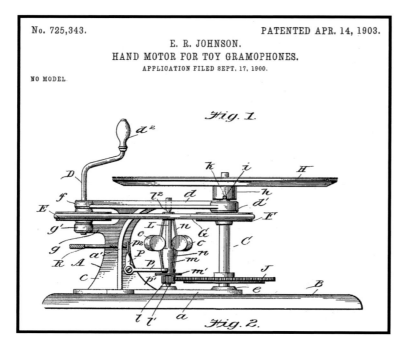

1901 Victor Toy Gramophone. Robin & Joan Rolfs Collection. (Value A)

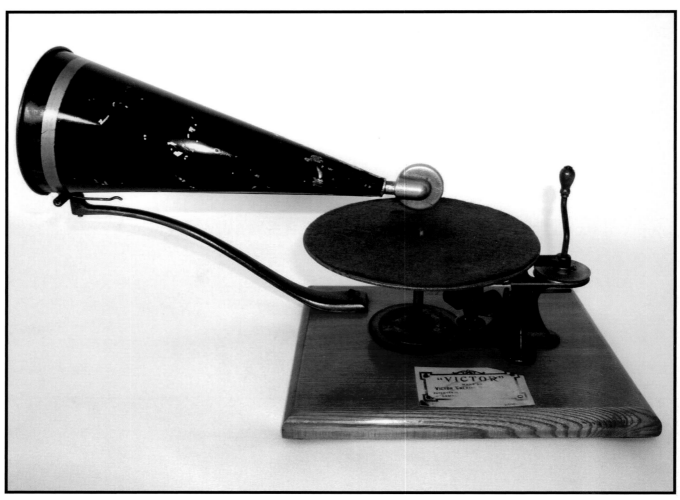

No. 725,343.   PATENTED APR. 14, 1903.

E. R. JOHNSON.
HAND MOTOR FOR TOY GRAMOPHONES.
APPLICATION FILED SEPT. 17, 1900.

NO MODEL.

Fig. 1.

Fig. 2.

VICTOR TOY GRAMOPHONE

By 1901, Eldridge Johnson was using the name "Victor" on several models of gramophones including the "Toy Victor." It wasn't until October 3, 1901 that the Victor Talking Machine Company was formed. This Victor Toy has a celluloid tag (Victor Talking Machine Co.) and a more refined horn support rather than the crude rod support utilized in the Toy Gramophone of 1900.

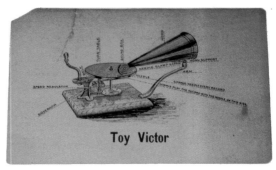

Instruction Card For Toy Victor. (Value F)

VICTOR TOY GRAMOPHONE - NIPPER DECAL

There appear to be at least three versions of the Toy Gramophone. The neat thing about this Toy Gramophone is the decal on the horn. It is a very colorful Nipper decal. The large gear on the turntable shaft is not fiber but is steel. Additionally there is no tag and never was one on the base. The rod horn support extends to the middle of the horn. This Toy Gramophone is as desirable for adult collectors today as it was for children of past generations.

Victor Toy Gramophone - Nipper Decal on Horn.
Shawn & Beth O'Rourke Collection. (Value A)

Note the unique Nipper and Gramophone decal on the horn. The U.S. Patent Office issued this TRADE MARK FOR GRAMOPHONE (34890) on July 10, 1900 to Emile Berliner, a citizen, residing at 1717 "P" Street N.W. Washington, D.C. and doing business at 1023 Twelfth Street, N.W., for his "Sound Reproducing Machines, their Appurtenances and Records." The original painting was conceived by Francis Barraud in 1899. The painting was sold to the Gramophone Company Ltd. for 50 pounds.

THE JOHNSON "TOY" RECORD

The 7 inch record included with the Toy Gramophone contained six selections for children. This was the first double-sided record to be sold to the public. The recording was made by William F. Hooley on November 6, 1900 (marked on the record 11/7/00) and was available for a year. Two variations of the "Toy" record are known. One has a Johnson Improved label on both sides (A-490; A-491) and the second carries a Victor Label on one side (A-490), and a V. T. M. Co. Victor Monarch label which drops the A- prefix, on the other side (491). This record has major historical importance due to the fact it was recorded on both sides. It would be another eight years before this two sided format would become the standard for disc records for the next eight decades.

The following is a transcript of this historic record.

A-490: "Now, dear children, Uncle Will will read to you about Old King Cole. Old King Cole was a merry old soul, ha ha ha ha ha, merry old soul was he. He called for his pipe, and he called for his glass, and he called for his fiddlers three. Sing a song a sixpence, a bag full of rye, four and twenty blackbirds baked in a pie, when the pie was opened the birds began to sing, wasn't that a dainty dish to set before a King? The King was in his counting-house, counting out his money. The Queen was in the parlor, eating bread and honey. The maid was in the garden hanging out the clothes, by came a little bird and snapped off her nose, ha ha ha ha. Now, dear children, Uncle Harry will sing you a little song. (with piano) Little Bo Peep has lost her sheep and can't know where to find them. Leave them alone and they'll come home and carry their tails behind them. Little Bo Peep is fast asleep and dreamt she heard them bleating, but when she awoke she found it a joke for still they were all sleeping. Now children, listen to the band. (cornet & piano)."

A-491/491: "Now, children, Uncle Will will read to you Mother Goose rhymes. Quack, quack, quack, quack, quack. Goosey goosey gander, whither shall I wander? Upstairs or downstairs or in my lady's chamber? There I met an old man who would not say his prayers so I took him by the left leg and threw him down the stairs. Baaa, Baaa, black sheep have you any wool? Yes sir, Yes sir, three bags full. One for my master and one for my dame and one for the little boy that lives in our lane. Little Jackie Horner sat in a corner eating a Christmas pie. He put in his thumb and took out a plum, and said, "What a good little boy am I." Now children, Uncle Harry will sing you a nice little song (with piano) London Bridge is falling down, my fair lady. Three blind mice, three blind mice, see how they run, see how they run. They all ran after the farmer's wife. She cut off their tails with a carving knife. Did you ever see such a sight in your life as three blind mice. Now children listen to the band. (At a Georgia Camp Meeting)."

Improved Record "A Record For The Children"
A-490/A-491 Label was the Same on Both Sides of Record.
Lawrence A. Schlick Collection. (Value E)

1901 Victor Seven Inch Two Sided Record With Victor Record Label on Side A-490 and Victor Monarch Record Label on Side 491.
Robin & Joan Rolfs Collection. (Value E)

Eureka Phonograph and Stollwerck Phonograph. Rene Rondeau Collection. (Value C)

STOLLWERCK & EUREKA "CHOCOLATE PHONOGRAPHE"

Eureka 1904 Laminated Records in Mailing Box.
Rene Rondeau Collection. (Value D)

Everyone loves chocolate. This was true throughout the ages. Henri Lioret promoted the phonograph as a mechanism used in chocolate advertising displays. Menier's Chocolate used the "Lioretgraph" to speak their slogan in a counter display. In 1903 two small phonographs were designed to play disc records made of chocolate! These phonographs and delicious records were sold in Belgium and Germany by the Stollwerck Chocolate Company, and in France by the French partner, Kratz-Boussac in the store Félix Potin under the brand name "Eureka." Both petite machines are identical except for the Stollwerck markings being absent on the Eureka. It was a clever way to increase chocolate sales, but these phonographs were extremely fragile and few have survived the past century.

The Stollwerck and Eureka phonographs were very small and measured a mere 8 1/2 inches tall including the horn. The turntable was 3 inches in diameter. The phonographs were powered by a tiny clock motor made by Junghans Clock Company, which is still in business today. This small phonograph with chocolate records would appeal to children. In a French magazine, *La Nature*, it was described as a phonograph and not a toy. They stated this phonograph is a solid machine which rivals more expensive phonographs. "It speaks sound, it sings well, and reproduces all songs with clarity."

Eureka Phonographe with Box. Rene Rondeau Collection. (Value C)

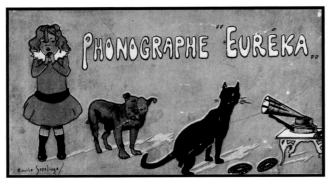

Eureka Phonographe Box Top.

The Eureka phonograph was packaged in a colorful box. It was the Phonographe Eureka! A black cat, dog and little girl eagerly await the the sound and the confectionary delight of the small Eureka Chocolate Records.

Original Print Showing the Eureka Phonographe. Rene Rondeau Collection.

Stollwerck Wood Base Phonographe. Rene Rondeau Collection. (Value C)

There were two basic types of phonographs produced by Stollwerck. The first models were constructed of delicately lithographed tin in green with gold decorations or reddish brown with gold trim. A later 1904 version has a carved oak case with brass hardware and a brass-belled horn with wood grain-painted body to match the color of the base. The removable turntable actually served as a storage compartment, holding three of the pre-recorded chocolate discs. The later wooden phonograph has a base measuring only 6 1/4 inches long by 4 3/4 inches wide, and only 2 inches tall.   The 1904 Stollwerck had a stronger motor with a separate speed control. It had a wood grained horn with a brass bell. The turntable and a majority of the other parts of this tiny phonograph were brass. The winding key fit through a hole in the turntable. This was an improvement over the early tin Stollwerck phonograph that was wound from underneath. A sapphire point in this improved phonograph replaced the glass stylus of the tin model. Larger records were offered for this new improved model. The records were 4 3/4 inches rather than 3 inches in diameter. They were made of a pressed wood composition with a very thin coating of a wax-like material. They were unbreakable and could not be eaten; however the surface tended to delaminate and chip. The earlier tin Stollwerck phonographs played chocolate records and more permanent records made out of a non-edible wax call "karbin" for a more permanent recording.   Five thousand of the new improved Stollwerck phonographs were sold.   These phonographs were fragile, noisy, had an underpowered motor and the songs were not reproduced with clarity. They were an excellent market for the chocolate records yet did not sell very well and the venture was a costly failure for the company. As the French Magazine, *La Nature* explained, "When a song no longer pleases, oh well! Just savor the disc like you would a simple snack, and eat it."

Bebe Jumeau Doll in Original Dress and Box. Julien Anton Collection. (Value A)

BEBE JUMEAU PHONOGRAPHE DOLL

The Edison phonograph doll was first shown at the 1889 Universal Exhibition in Paris among other great inventions of the inventor, Thomas A. Edison. A.T.E. Wangemann, an assistant of Mr. Edison, had brought over from America a prototype of the doll. Emile Jumeau visited the Exhibition and after viewing the Edison doll wanted to add speech to his Bebe. One day he brought a doll to Henri Lioret and asked him to make it talk. Henri Lioret was a successful clock maker. He had been born into a clock making family and had spent four years in college studying about his trade, so at the age of forty-five he was well established in his career. Emile Jumeau was a successful doll maker known throughout France. Jumeau & Liroet had the perfect combination of talents to make a French talking doll.

In *Mon Journal*, a children's publication of the date September 2, 1893, an advertisement appeared: "Most of you probably own Jumeau dolls since they are the most sought-after by little girls; but didn't you ever wish your dolls could speak, laugh and sing? Well, you won't need to wish any more. The Bebe Jumeau Phonograph will soon make its debut, thanks to a wonderful invention, the fruit of much research and testing which have fortunately paid off after long labor. This invention will revolutionize little girl's toys." However, the greatest difficulty was in allowing the Bebe Jumeau phonograph to vary its conversation.

"In order to create a repertoire for her, we have created this competition, in association with the Jumeau firm, which always seeks to please its young clientele. The readers of *Mon Journal* are invited to enter phrases they would like to hear spoken by their dolls..." Of course, the winner of the competition was to receive one of the first dolls scheduled to come out the end of 1893. On December 9, 1893, an illustrated article in the children's scientific journal *La Nature*, introduced the talking doll.

Henri Lioret learned from the failure of Edison's Doll. He wanted interchangeable cylinders strong enough to stand up to the manipulation by children. By 1893, his first phonograph was working. It was small, manually driven and had a resonator made of a cylindrical cardboard box with a horn on top. His first patent was dated May 18, 1893. Jumeau wanted to commercialize his new doll before Christmas and selected a model that was 25 inches tall.

Catalog Advertisement Showing the Bebe Doll and Clockwork Motor. Julien Anton Collection. (Value H)

Lioret "Le Merveilleux" Phonographe. Rene Rondeau Collection. (Value B)

A toy phonograph was marketed in 1894 by Henri Lioret. The same mechanism as used in the Bebe Jumeau doll body was put into a small cardboard case and marketed as "Le Merveilleux" (The Marvelous). It played cylinders running about 30 seconds each. Many of the titles were children's songs; however a variety of other titles were offered. The mechanism is a wire frame, conventional clock spring, and fan governor. The reproducer was made with a cardboard sound chamber, mica diaphragm, and bent steel stylus. The horn was a celluloid cone pointed upwards.

Lioret "Le Merveilleux" Phonographe. Rene Rondeau Collection. (Value B)

Bebe Jumeau Doll Cylinder.
Robin & Joan Rolfs Collection. (Value G)

Bebe Jumeau Cylinder Catalog. Julien Anton Collection.
(Value G)

Lioret began experimenting and had a celluloid cylinder patented on November 28, 1893 (Supplement to Patent 230177 of May 18, 1893). He patented a process of recording on celluloid. He immersed the cylinder in hot water or camphorated alcohol to soften it prior to recording, which allowed the stylus to record on the celluloid. These cylinders were fine grooved recordings. The record had a brass core and was very durable. Purchasers could select recordings containing narratives or songs for the doll. In 1893 the Bebe phonograph doll was advertised as a talking, singing doll that could hold a conversation of thirty-five words. In 1894 with the additional cost of 70 cents, the conversation could be recorded in French, English or Spanish. Because the doll was so beautiful and the phonograph worked so well, people would gladly pay the 49 francs for the Bebe Jumeau Phonographe doll.

Jumeau published a catalogue containing the repertoire found on the cylinder, in several languages:
-In French (no. 1-17, green white and red label)
-In Spanish (no. 101-109, yellow label)
-In English (no. 201-209, red label)
-In Russian (no. 301-309)

The text of each nursery rhyme or monologue, recorded by a performer with a childlike voice, was printed on the cylinder label. No. 7 is rare and touching. It recounts the doll's creation: "I dreamed that Santa Claus brought me a pretty Bebe Jumeau who speaks, laughs, and sings just like me."

The Bebe phonograph cylinders may need to be cleaned. It is suggested that a gentle wiping with a soft cloth dipped in olive oil will clean and lubricate the celluloid surface.

Bebe Jumeau is 26 inches tall with a bisque head, pierced ears and paperweight eyes. Paperweight eyes means that they were made of glass and blown similarly to antique paperweights. She has a delicate open mouth with beautiful teeth. The original long human hair wigs were of various colors. This exquisite French doll, like the Edison doll, could be purchased with simple dress for 39 francs or stylish silk French dress for 49 francs.

Bebe Jumeau Doll in Fancy Dress.
Warren E. Kelm Collection. (Value A)

Bebe Jumeau Doll Shown With Plain Dress in Box.
Warren E. Kelm Collection. (Value A)

The doll's body is made of paper mache with an opening in the front for the phonograph works. The arms and legs are of carved wood with ball joints. In 1891 Emile Jumeau registered a French trademark to be stamped on Jumeau shoes. Bebe Jumeau's fashions are a selection of a simplistic dress with a pattern of small flowers of blue or red on a white background. A more luxurious dress is in "surah" silk and was more expensive in the Lioret catalog (+10 francs). Both dresses have a turned-down flap that allows access to the mechanism for changing the cylinder.

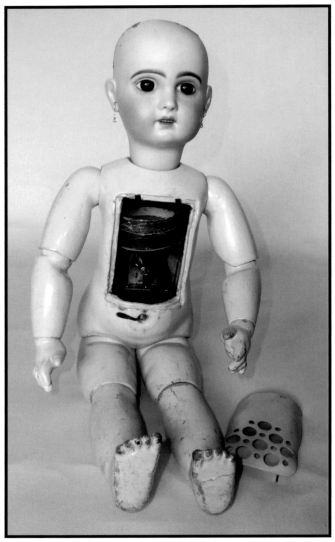

Bebe Jumeau Doll Body.
Robin & Joan Rolfs Collection. (Value C)

Jumeau Trademark "Depose TETE JUMEAU"
on Head of Doll.

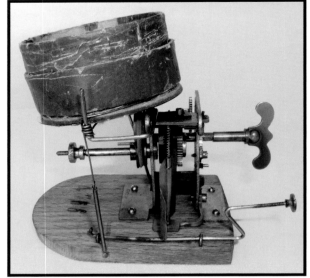

Bebe Jumeau Motor.

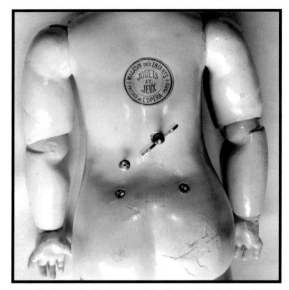

Trademark, Store Label, & Key on Back of Doll.

The head was marked "Depose Tete Jumeau" with the number 11. Sometimes the head was replaced with a newer head which was made after 1899. When it was marked "DEPOSE JUMEAU," this head was made by SFBJ, the successors of the company after its bankruptcy. If no mark is found or it is different from the aforementioned marks, the head is made by an after market manufacturer. The Lioret trademark is also shown on the phonograph parts. The mechanism is found in the chest of the doll. It has a removable metal or fiber chest plate to gain access to the mechanism. A winding key projects from the center of the back, together with a plunger to start and stop the motor. An air vane governor allowing the doll to sing and talk without manual assistance is controlled by the spring-operated motor. The Jumeau phonograph doll was marketed from 1894 to 1900. Lioret promoted various phonograph mechanisms used in advertising displays, in clocks, and finally developed a precision Lioret phonograph. This French doll definitely makes more than a fashion statement. The Jumeau doll has the honor of being the first French phonograph as well as the first spring-operated mechanism with interchangeable, unbreakable celluloid cylinders.

Early Arnoldia Doll. Robin & Joan Rolfs Collection. (Value B)

Early Arnoldia Doll Motor Front View.

Early Arnoldia Doll Motor Side View.

ARNOLDIA DOLL

The Arnoldia doll is the largest of the early phonograph dolls. This is a large doll measuring 80 cm. (31 1/2 inches) with a natural hair wig. This German talking doll uses a cylinder mechanism that plays wax cylinders much like the early cylinder phonographs of the day. The cylinder phonograph mechanism found inside this incredible German doll is a well-constructed precision mechanism employing an automatic return and shutoff device. Its mechanics somewhat resembles that of a coin operated mechanism. The maker of the Arnoldia doll was Max Oscar Arnold of Neustadt, Germany. Mr. Arnold specialized in mechanical dolls. In 1904, he obtained his first British and French patents for a mechanical doll. This doll moved on wheels, alternately saying "Mama" and "Papa" while turning its head, opening and closing its eyes and swinging its arms forward and backward. After this mechanical marvel, he became interested in phonograph dolls. Thus, Arnold patented a phonograph doll in 1906 with German and British patents and a French patent in 1907.

Front View of Later Arnoldia Motors.

It is known that there are two and possibly three different models of this doll. All have a jointed composition body. The earliest model has the tin phonograph horn passing through the neck, projecting upward. The bisque head has openings at the back and top allowing the sound to escape. The head fits snuggly onto the torso with no mechanical attachment. A variation of this model incorporates a mechanical connection via a rod from the motor to the eyes. While playing, the eyes move as she sings and talks! It should be noted that the body could be separated above the hips. The phonograph mechanism is mounted on a wooden platform placed in the trunk of the body. The mandrel is made out of wood and the spring motor is key wound. In 1908, Arnold obtained another patent in Great Britain and Germany for further improvements, one of which was making a metal front on the body for a speaker. This second model has a small horn bent to the front, which allows the sound to exit the chest. This doll was smaller in size and used a cylinder of a shorter length. A third and smaller version of the Arnold mechanism exists. Similar to the second model with the forward horn, this machine is smaller in size and has a shorter mandrel.

Arnoldia Doll Later Model.
Domenic DiBernardo Collection. (Value B)

Third and Smaller Variation of Compact
Arnoldia Doll Motor. Jean-Paul Agnard Collection.

Second Model of Arnoldia Doll Motor.
Jean-Paul Agnard Collection.

Although not shown on the patent drawing, the production of the motor for all models retained the vestiges of an earlier version of a doll that had a mechanical linkage to the eyes. When operated, a cam activated a lever that connected a wire to the eyes making them move up and down as the doll spoke. Visible on the side is the lever mechanism on an early motor. The crescent shaped opening accesses the cam. The same shaped opening can be seen on previous images of the doll motors.

Mechanism to Activate the Eyes of the Arnoldia Doll. Jean-Paul Agnard Collection.

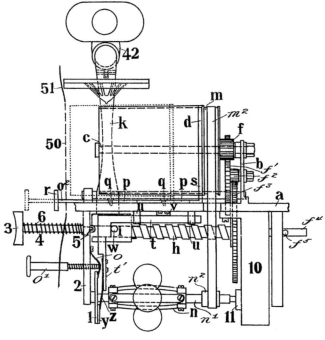

U. S. Patent Granted to Max Oscar Arnold for "Phonograph".

Arnola Doll Record in Box. Jean-Paul Agnard Collection. (Value G)

ARNOLDIA DOLL CYLINDERS

The Arnoldia doll played cylinders recorded in German, English, Spanish and French languages. The 200 series cylinders are German, the 400 series English, the 600 series French and 800 series Spanish. The wax cylinders were recorded with 100 threads per inch and would fit on a standard cylinder talking machine mandrel. The cylinders have an outside diameter of 55 mm. (2 1/8 in.) and the length of 60 mm. (2 5/16 in). Shorter cylinders may exist. The cylinders are not titled, but do have a number corresponding to the catalog number and title printed on the lid of the record box. Each box has a green label which states: "Edison - Gesellschaft mbm." It is believed that the Excelsior Company in Kolonia, Germany made them under Edison patents. There are also doll records marketed under the Arnola Record label.

Arnoldia Doll Cylinders. Robin & Joan Rolfs Collection. (Value G)

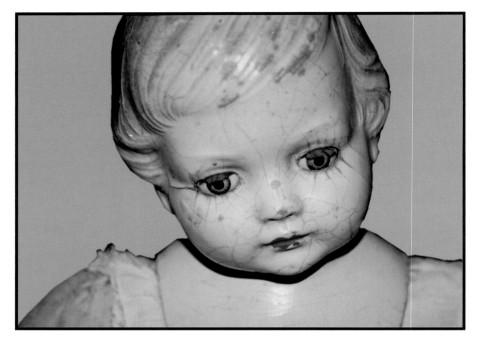

K and K 23 Inch Phonograph Doll
and Motor in Back of Doll.
John & Carole Mehling Collection. (Value E)

K AND K DOLL

K and K represented the doll makers George Kolb and Fred Kolb. This company was in business from 1915 to 1925. They were owned and controlled by Geo. Borgfeldt and Company of 48-50 W. 4th Street, New York. The K and K phonograph doll is twenty-three inches long with a cloth body and composition head and arms. The face has expressive blue sleep eyes and real lashes. Her light brown hair is molded. The doll's head is unique because it swivels on the shoulder base. Found inside the head is a round wire attachment for the rubber tube that is connected to the reproducer. This rubber tube amplifies the sound that comes out of the top of the doll's head. The phonograph works are similar to those found in the earliest Madame Hendren Doll.

The motor mechanism is rather unique. It is a clockwork motor that is 3 inches wide and 4 3/4 inches long. On the mechanism is stamped "Pat. Apld For." A gear train of four gears turns the mandrel that connects via a belt to a cam and lever mechanism that positions the stylus to the beginning of the record at the end of play. An air vane governor controls the motor speed. She plays cylinder records that are celluloid over a cardboard core that is 2 1/8 inches in diameter and 1 1/4 inches in length. The hue of the cylinder varies from dark navy blue to black. They are open at both ends and difficult for a child to insert into the doll. The main spring can be wound tight with a key with just one revolution. The steel stylus is located 1/4 inch above the beginning of the record. When the winding key is removed from the mandrel, the stylus moves to the beginning of the record and plays the entire record. After the recording has finished, the stylus moves back to the original position at the start of the record. The stylus is located about 2 1/8 inches below the stationary diaphragm. A fine steel wire connects the stylus to the center of the diaphragm. The sound is clear and comes from the top of the head of the doll. The entire mechanism is housed in a wood box, which is then placed in the body of the doll.

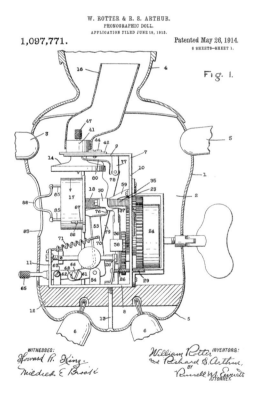

Early 1913 Doll Mechanism by William Rotter and Richard Arthur Incorporates Principles Found in the K and K Doll and Later Averill Products.

Combination Rastus and Boxers. Robin & Joan Rolfs Collection. (Value F)

RAGTIME RASTUS AND BOXERS

The phonograph was the major center of entertainment in the 1900's. To add to the amazement of the phonograph, toys were added for the interest of the audience. The National Toy Company conceived of a phonograph toy named Ragtime Rastus. He was patented on March 16, 1915. Rastus skipped and tapped out a dance to a 78 rpm record to the delight of children and adults alike. Rastus is 5 1/2 inches high with jointed knees, hips and shoulders. His feet lightly tapped on a wooden platform on which he was loosely suspended by a stiff piece of wire. The mechanism that made Rastus dance was below the platform that fitted over a spindle of the record turntable. As the spindle turned, the wire that supported Rastus was rapidly raised and lowered, with a skipping action and clicking noise. A small wooden adapter ring coupled the device to the turntable spindle. The imprint "National Toy Co." and patent dates are found on the underside of the platform. Fighting Boxing Darkies were often sold in combination with Rastus to entertain the sports fans listening to the phonograph.

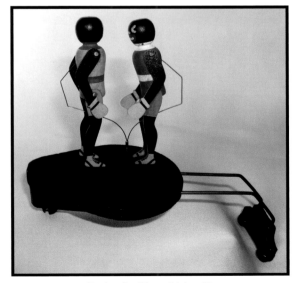

Boxing Darkies. (Value G)

RAGTIME RASTUS VARIATIONS

Ragtime Rastus remained the most popular figure of the dancing phonograph toys. The Columbia Graphophone Company also had its own variation of Ragtime Rastus made by the National Toy Company. The Columbia Rastus had wood arms rather than pressed cardboard. The box cover also noted that it was distributed by the Columbia Graphophone Company of New York. Rastus was shown dancing atop a Columbia tabletop phonograph.

The dapper dancer pictured uses the same platform made by the National Toy Co. The platforms are imprinted with the name "National Toy Co. Boston, Mass. U.S.A." and a Patent date of March 16, 1915.

"Dancing Sam The Famous Dancer" was another variation of the mechanical dancer made by the Dancing Sam Novelty Company of Cleveland, Ohio. The mechanism was simpler and cheaper.

Unidentified Dancing Rastus. (Value F)

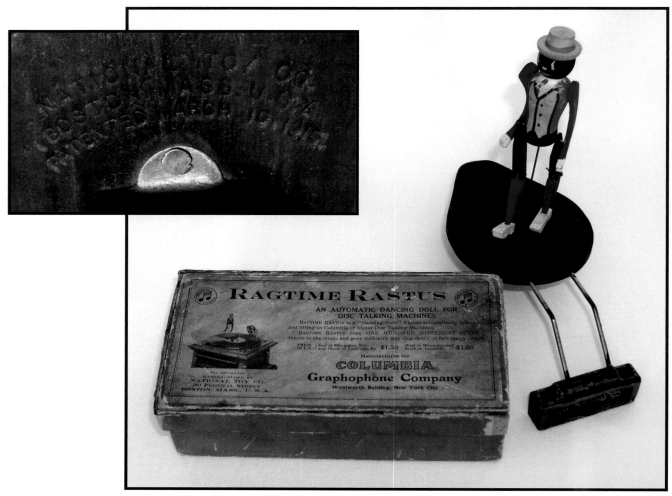

Ragtime Rastus by Columbia Graphophone Company. Robin & Joan Rolfs Collection. (Value F)

SHIMANDY & FIGHTING ROOSTERS

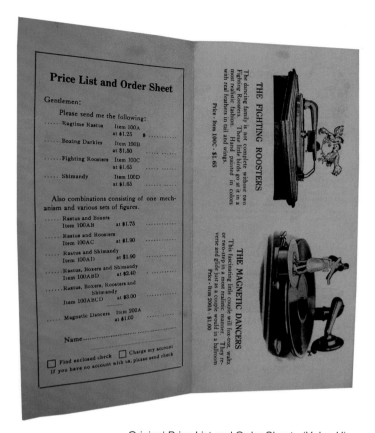

Price List and Order Sheet

Gentlemen:

Please send me the following:

..... Ragtime Rastus   Item 100A
                        at $1.25 $ ....

..... Boxing Darkies   Item 100B
                        at $1.50   ....

..... Fighting Roosters Item 100C
                        at $1.65   ....

..... Shimandy   Item 100D
                        at $1.65   ....

Also combinations consisting of one mechanism and various sets of figures.

..... Rastus and Boxers
      Item 100AB   at $1.75   ....

..... Rastus and Roosters
      Item 100AC   at $1.90   ....

..... Rastus and Shimandy
      Item 100AD   at $1.90   ....

..... Rastus, Boxers and Shimandy
      Item 100ABD   at $2.40   ....

..... Rastus, Boxers, Roosters and
      Shimandy
      Item 100ABCD at $3.00   ....

..... Magnetic Dancers   Item 200A
                         at $1.00 ....

Name...

☐ Find enclosed check   ☐ Charge my account
If you have no account with us, please send check

THE FIGHTING ROOSTERS

The dancing family is not complete without two Fighting Roosters. These little birds go at it in a most realistic fashion. Hand painted in colors with real feathers in tail and wings.

Price - Item 100C - $1.65

THE MAGNETIC DANCERS

This fascinating little couple will fox-trot, waltz or two-step in a most realistic manner. They reverse and glide just as a couple would in a ballroom.

Price - Item 200A - $1.00

Original Price List and Order Sheet. (Value H)

Shimandy Phonograph Toy. (Value F)

The National Toy Company may have felt that Rastus needed a partner. In August of 1921 Shimandy, a female dancer was added to the lineup. She wore a classy silk dress. This dancing partner sold for $2.50. She was more expensive than Rastus. Perhaps it was because of her fashionable dress, hat and ivory colored shoes.

A scarce figure from the National Toy Company is a colorful pair of fighting roosters. They are known to lose their feathers in the fight. All figures were designed by Walter Balke, for the National Toy Company, located at 167 Oliver Street in Boston. The toys were sold through the stores of F.A.O. Schwarz, Gimbels Bros., Jordan Marsh, and Wm. Filene as well as Victor and Columbia Talking Machine dealers. It was reported that over 8,800 of these toys were sold between January and June 1916 and the company was producing 15,000 more during the remainder year of 1916.

Fighting Roosters. Robin & Joan Rolfs Collection. (Value F)

1 - 35

UNCLE SAM
PHONOGRAPH TOYS

It was wartime and Uncle Sam was a very popular figure. It was also the time of wartime prohibition. Uncle Sam was fighting the "Demon Rum" in the shape of a whiskey bottle, with a snake coming out of the neck of the bottle. Of course Uncle Sam always won the fight! This dancer retailed for $1.75.

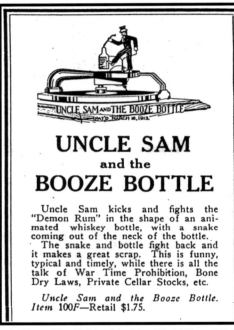

Ad From *The Talking Machine World* Circa 1918. (Value I)

Other dancers also reflected the politics of the day. One such figure was "Uncle Sam Kicking the Kaiser." Another 1916 figure was "Uncle Sam Kicking Pancho Villa." These dance figures sold from $1.25 to $3.00. You could purchase combinations consisting of one mechanism and various sets of figures for a greater savings. They all came in the same box with different designations of the item stamped on the top of the box.

Uncle Sam Kicking Pancho Villa. (Value E)

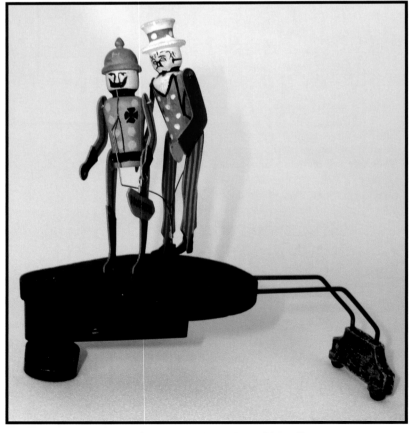

Uncle Sam Kicking The Kaiser. (Value E)

1 - 36

Two Versions of The Tango Two Dancers, British Made. Robin & Joan Rolfs Collection. (Value G)

MAGNETIC DANCERS

Magnetic Dancers, American Made.
Scott Malawski Collection. (Value F)

In 1922 the National Toy Company introduced another phonograph toy. It consisted of cardboard figures in ballroom dress called the "Magnetic Dancers." The two-dimensional figures were held upright by a metal clip on a small tin template that is placed on a round brass platform. The center axle is magnetized and attracts the edge of the tin template. Different templates produce different dance steps such as the fox trot, waltz or tango. As the appropriate music plays, the figures dance to the music. The National Toy Company apparently conceived of the idea from England. The English toy was called "The Tango Two" and was patented on January 6, 1920. There are two boxes of the English version, both labeled "Tango Two." The National Toy Company listed the English patent as well as its own patent in August 1922. The American box portrays the couple dancing on an internal horn Columbia Grafonola and is titled "The Magnetic Dancers."

CHARLESTON'S DANCERS

These Charleston's celluloid dancers will dance their way into your heart. Charlie Chaplin, Cupid, and others with their hands in their pockets twirl around on a platform of tin. The platform is similar to the National Toy Company platform, but varies in shape. Toys with original boxes command a higher price. The Charleston's Dancers is a French phonograph toy.

The Charleston's Dancers, Charlie Chaplin. Howard Hazelcorn Collection. (Value E)

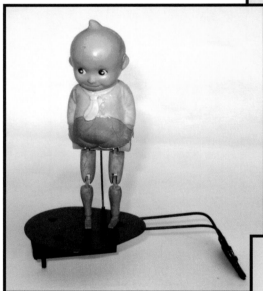

Dancing Cupid. (Value F)

PICKETT'S PHONO FIGURES

This red haired British girl dances on top of a wood platform. She is 7 inches tall. This toy is driven by the rim of the turntable. As the turntable turns, the brightly colored girl wiggles and dances to a catchy tune of the day.

Pickett's Phono Figure. Howard Hazelcorn Collection. (Value E)

SIAM SOO

The most complicated phonograph toy is called "Siam Soo." She is like a three-dimensional marionette doll in full dress. As the ad states: "Siam Soo: She puts the Oh!-Oh! in Graf-o-nola!" This toy was made by the Morton E. Converse & Son Co. of Winchendon, Massachusetts and sold exclusively by the Columbia Graphophone Co. The date that manufacturing commenced is uncertain (1917-1921). Siam Soo is 11 1/2 inches high. She is one of the largest phonograph toys made in America. Siam Soo's movements are very intricate and lifelike. She certainly demands the attention of the viewer. She has a wood hand-painted face. Her headdress is scarlet red with gold ornamentation. Her 5 1/2 inch length skirt came in three different prints. They were a basic camel colored skirt, a daring red and black plaid and another is a beautiful colored paisley print. The skirt is held around her waist with a drawstring.

There is a 1919 patent date on the box, but this is misleading. Another date of 1909 appears on the label on the base of Siam Soo. This patent was issued to George L. Hall of Weatherford, Texas. The other patents for Siam Soo were awarded to John M. Foster of Fulton NY (1919) and to Atherton D. Converse (1923). The manufacturer of Siam Soo was Morton E. Converse and Co. They specialized in manufacturing hobbyhorses, toy trunks and drums. They had their own in-house color lithograph presses. There were two styles of boxes. A cardboard box with wood ends mailed the Columbia Siam Soo to her destination. Later boxes were entirely of cardboard and all were ornately decorated. The brown paper mailing wrapper was also printed with advertising about Siam Soo and her famous dances.

Siam Soo With Original Shipping Box. Robin & Joan Rolfs Collection. (Value E)

In 1921, Atherton D. Converse filed a U.S. patent for a dancing doll. This earlier model has folding legs with counter-balanced spring tension screws to support the wooden block above the turntable. The metal support that centers the mechanism on the turntable spindle is a fairly substantial metal strap. The later version has two rigid 1/4 inch diameter steel rods with adjustable rubber cups. These steel rods or legs needed to be unscrewed to pack Siam Soo in her colorful box. The metal centering bracket is lightweight steel prone to breakage. The forearms of the doll are joined to each other in a raised position with a small bent wire, looped in the middle. A black and white cord runs through the head and controls the motion of her hands. Her head turns, her torso moves and her arms move up and down. All this wiggling action is generated by a three inch metal and rubber wheel that makes perpendicular contact with the record label surface. This gives Siam Soo the energy to dance via a hidden rigid wire behind the doll.

Earlier Version of Columbia Siam Soo. Scott Malawski Collection. (Value E)

Each box suggests an appropriate record catalogue number and title to be played with the dancing doll. The earlier box for the doll with folding legs lists 27 records and 28 titles (one number listed twice with alternate sides). The later box lists 18 records and 36 titles. Six records are listed on both boxes but not all record numbers correspond to their respective titles. The record titled *Siam Soo* by The Happy Six is not listed on either box.

A short story is found on the boxes which accounts for Converse's entry into the Siamese doll business:

> "An American traveler in Siam visited the King's Harem and was attracted by the unusual motions of the King's dancers. A model was made by a Siamese toy maker and adapted by Morton E. Converse & Son Company to play on the Columbia Grafonola--or any other disc phonograph. The dancers in the King's Harem have their frocks gilded to indicate royalty and their faces are covered with a heavy paste to conceal any facial emotions, this depending solely on the motions of the dance. Siam Soo is true to all these details and the motion of her dancing is strikingly similar to that of the Royal Siamese Dancers in the King's Harem."

A Columbia record was released May 1921 entitled *"Siam Soo."* The music was by Otto Motzan and M. K. Jerome and lyrics by Sidney F. Lazarus. Yerkes Happy Six recorded it on February 8, 1931, with a vocal by Frank Crumit; catalog number A3379. Only one take was released and it was backed with the Hawaiian Blues selection, *"Make Believe."* Some believe the record is as rare as the Siam Soo doll. The 10 inch blue-label record was advertised in the Columbia Catalog for at least a year and sold for 85 cents. If you want Siam Soo to dance on her record, be aware that care should be taken to protect the label area. The wheel that makes Siam Soo dance can damage the record label. Siam Soo made a significant impact on the talking machine toy market.

Siam Soo Record. (Value G)

PHONOGRAPH TOP

This phonograph 4 1/2 inch top spins a tune. It had four songs, *Houtchie Kouchie; Yankee Doodle; Home, Sweet Home; and Dixie.* A paper cone was the reproducer. The top has dimples arranged in a concentric pattern and when the end of the paper cone is touched to the rapidly spinning top, a humming or buzzing sound is produced. Moving the cone in or out will vary the pitch. About five seconds of playing time can be expected. Extra cones were five for ten cents. If you tired of playing a tune, the child could put on six different colored record designs for his or her amusement. The phonograph top was manufactured by Ralph P. Harlan, Dept. 87, Chicago, Ill.

Phonograph Top. (Value H)

French Block Phonograph Puzzle
Shown with Nine of the Blocks Placed on Top of the Storage Box. (Value G)

PHONOGRAPH PUZZLE

Children and the amazing phonograph are depicted on this 10 1/4 x 13 inch wood block puzzle. This French puzzle from the 1900s is made up of forty-eight blocks measuring 1 1/2 inches each. It is six puzzles in one. Each side of the wooden blocks forms a Victorian children's scene. The blocks are stored in a wooden box with the children and phonograph printed on the cover. There is also a smaller version of this puzzle. It appears that an enterprising young man is demonstrating the new invention of the talking machine to his eager audience. Not everyone present seems to be enthused with the sound of the phonograph. This is indeed puzzling.

Penny Phonograph. (Value F)

Penny Tin Gramophone. (Value G)

PHONOGRAPH
PENNY TOYS

For one penny children could purchase a "Penny Gramophone." This 3 1/2 inch miniature tin toy actually played. By winding the crank it plucked a few notes on a crude teeth mechanism inside the phonograph. Another miniature penny toy was a Toy Phonograph that plucked a cylinder. This intricate phonograph was very ornate and detailed.

EDISON TOYS

Edison Flyer Train. John & Frances Wiedey Collection. (Value F)

A wooden Edison Flyer train could ride on tracks of imagination for boys and girls. They could travel on the "Edison River" car and view the sights. They came in red, blue and green colors.

Edison Little Folks Crib.
John & Frances Wiedey Collection. (Value G)

It was 1929 and Thomas A. Edison Phonographs were no longer in vogue and production ceased. Radios were replacing the once popular phonographs. Thomas Edison sent a young man by the name of Thomas Fitzgerald to New London, Wisconsin to change a factory that manufactured phonograph cabinets into a factory that would make "Edison Little Folks Furniture." They designed and manufactured rocking chairs, doll beds, child's table and chair sets for the little folks to play house. They specialized in nursery and juvenile furniture. "Little Folks" furniture was made in New London, Wisconsin at the Edison Plant until the factory closed in 2004. Today cribs and juvenile furniture are manufactured under the Simmons brand name with the "Little Folks" decal found on the quality furniture pieces.

CHAPTER 2

DOLLS & TOYS OF THE ROARING 1920s -1940s

It was the roaring 1920s and the music was happy and carefree. For the first time women were voting and cutting their hair in a short bob style. It was a time to enjoy life and dance the Charleston, Black Bottom, Lindy Hop, Collegiate and Breakaway and to embrace a new type of music called jazz. The Madame Hendren doll wore her flapper headband, talked and sang to the children of the 1920s. The Victrola School House phonograph was endorsed by educators and used in more than 25,000 public schools. The phonograph became part of a child's everyday life at school and home. The toy manufacturers saw a market for phonograph toys to entertain children and adults alike.

Children and parents were selling magazines, newspapers and entering contests to win a talking Madame Hendren doll. In local newspapers, children sought to read a column by "The Doll Lady." They would see their name and the name of the doll they won in the Doll Lady Column. One such lucky girl was Mary Virginia Hill, of Clarksburg, West Virginia. In the Clarksburg, WV Telegram Newspaper the Doll Lady wrote the following about Mary Virginia and her phonograph doll. The title of the article was "Local Girls Get Wonder Dolls." The article featuring Mary Virginia's doll follows:

Mary Virginia Hill Pollard Age 2 With Her
Madame Hendren Doll Named Marjorie Daw. Circa 1926.

"Well, it's a good thing I sent for more of my dollies, because more of them are being taken from me by little girls hereabout, and many others in different parts of central West Virginia are working for them. Besides the ones which have been taken into new homes, others have been reserved, so the new family I ordered won't be getting here any too soon. But, don't worry, children. There'll be dolls for all of you. I can always see to that."

A PRETTY NAME

"Marjorie Daw is the name of one of the dollies that has found a new home. Isn't that sweet? Marjorie Daw has gone to make her home with little Mary Virginia Hill at 309 Rosemont Avenue. Mary Virginia is 2 years old. Her father is T.S. Hill, foreman of the Central Fireproof garage."

The article continued to list the names of little girls and the names of their adopted Madame Hendren dolls. The Doll Lady ended the article by saying: *"Don't forget to write me, children. I will be at the Telegram office all the week in Clarksburg. Come and see me, and I will tell you how simple and easy it is to earn one of these remarkable babies."*

Other little girls received their dolls for special occasions such as Christmas, birthdays or just for being a good girl. These dolls were purchased by their parents, grandparents or by a special aunt or uncle. Joan Mulligan of Milwaukee was one such lucky girl. It was Christmas Day 1925 when Joan first saw her grandmother and uncle walking into the room with her Madame Hendren between them playing the prayer *Now I Lay Me Down To Sleep*. Joan being the only grandchild was totally delighted. She still cherishes her Madame Hendren Doll today and recalls her grandmother telling her that she purchased her doll at Epstein's Department Store in Milwaukee for $25.00, a large sum of money in 1925.

Joan Mulligan With Her Madame Hendren Doll in Year 2004.

A prominent doll manufacturing company of the day was the Averill Manufacturing Co. Inc. that flourished from 1915 through 1925. This firm was founded in New York by Georgene Averill, her husband James Paul Averill and Rudolph A. Hopf, Georgene's brother. The reason this manufacturing company seemed to prevail in the competitive doll market of the 1920's is due, in part, to the patented Averill doll cylinder phonograph motor. This ubiquitous motor was successfully used not only by the Averill Company, but also by other doll manufacturers including the K & K Toy Co., EFFanBEE and others. Manufacturer confusion can easily result because this easily recognized motor was used in so many phonograph dolls known only by their copyrighted trade names. James Paul Averill and his wife Georgene left the Averill Manufacturing Co. in the 1920s and organized two other companies. One was Madame Georgene, Inc. of which Paul Averill was President. This was primarily a design firm to handle the doll designs created by Georgene Averill. The other company was Paul Averill, Inc. This was the distributing arm, which wholesaled and retailed the dolls. The Averill's worked closely with Borgfeldt, a large New York doll importer and distributor. The dolls were manufactured by the K & K Toy Co. factory, which was controlled by Borgfeldt. Several very successful dolls that were designed and marketed were the *Wonder Mama Dolls*, including *Mistress Bubbles, Master Bubbles, Billy Boy* and *Betty*. Advertisements stated: "They walk, they talk, they dance." These were not phonograph dolls, but "mama" dolls that used the Lloyd voice mechanism. These companies along with the original Averill Manufacturing Co. continued to produce the majority of dolls made in the U.S.A. Thus the success of the Averill's was a result of the prolific design talents of Georgene Averill and her husband's business capacity. Together they created a plethora of dolls, designs, patents, trade names and marketing agencies for their products that today result in confusion in identifying phonograph dolls of the 1920s.

A DOLL-CHILD FOR MY OWN

The Akron Evening Times has promised me that if I will get some new subscriptions for them, they will give me a Wonder Character Singing Doll. If you will take The Akron Evening Times from me, you will be getting the best paper in this part of the country and I will be getting my dolly.

SUBSCRIBER'S AGREEMENT. I am not now taking The Akron Evening Times and have not been for the last 30 days. I understand in filling out the blank below I agree to take The Akron Evening Times, Daily and Sunday for six months and thereafter until ordered discontinued, paying for paper at regular carrier rate, 18c per week in city, 19c per week in suburban towns.

I hereby pay $1.00 to be applied on subscription.

PLEASE FILL IN BLANK BELOW

Subscriber's Name _____

Address _____

Phone No. _____ Apt. _____

Order Taken by _____

Address _____

Akron Evening Times Subscription Agreement for Dolly-Rekord.

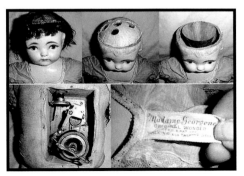

Madame Georgene Original Wonder Doll.
Jean-Paul Agnard Collection.   (Value E)

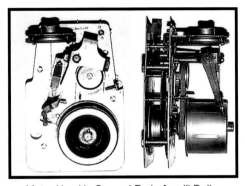

Motor Used in Several Early Averill Dolls.
Jean-Paul Agnard Collection.

MADAME GEORGENE ORIGINAL WONDER

The Madame Georgene's Original Wonder Doll was manufactured by the Averill Company. Georgene Averill organized the Averill Company as a family business in 1915, with her husband Paul Averill as head of the Averill Manufacturing Company. Georgene Averill was a New York doll designer. James Paul Averill was a buyer of toys for the Meier & French firm in New York. They manufactured and marketed dolls all designed and patented by Georgene Averill. By 1917, the company had grown to one hundred and twenty-five employees making thirty styles of baby dolls and two hundred and fifty styles of character dolls. The Madame Georgene doll has painted eyes with a composition head. A large horn occupies most of the space of the head, projecting the sound upward through large holes in the top of the dolls head. The cloth body houses the key wind motor that is accessed from the back. The motor is housed in a wooden box. The doll's dress is marked with a tag "Madame Georgene."

MADAME HENDREN

Madame Hendren was a trade name copyrighted by the Averill Manufacturing Company. Early in the formative years of the company, the idea of manufacturing a phonograph doll must have intrigued the Averill's. The basic shortcomings of earlier manufacturers of phonograph dolls were apparent. The motor mechanisms were often unreliable and sound was faint and often severely distorted by unregulated record speed. Handling the doll while it was playing would often send the stylus skating across the record. Records were difficult for a child to change and often subject to breakage. Motor size often precluded making the doll soft, cuddly and lovable. Above all, the prohibitive cost of developing a doll that could overcome any or all of these deficiencies doomed it for market failure.

A major turn of events occurred when a gentleman named Richard S. Arthur applied for several cylinder phonograph motor patents in 1917. Although it was likely, it is not known whether the New York resident was employed by the Averill's. He was granted the patents (1355523 and 1357936) in 1920. These patents were strictly designed to overcome deficiencies of earlier motors used in phonograph dolls. Specific claims of the patents addressed the problems of uneven record speed related to outside vibrations and movement of the mechanism. His small cylinder player employed a small self-contained worm driven governor consisting of weighted shoes fitted into a cylindrical housing. Its low mass allowed it to be effective under the stress of outside shock and movement. In addition, the cylinder mandrel was driven indirectly by a torsion spring mounted on the rotating mandrel shaft. This provided a yielding connection between the motor and the cylinder.

The reproducer was fixed at one location on a yoke which allowed it to pivot so the extended stylus could reach from beginning to end of the short 1 1/4 inch cylinder record. A hand operated rod worked a cam that would lower the stylus onto the beginning of the record and also turn the motor on and raise the stylus turning the motor off at the end of play. A leaf spring incorporated in the yoke assembly applied pressure to the stylus and prevented vibrations causing the stylus to skip. Motive power was derived from a wire spring coiled around the length of the winding shaft. The uniquely simple and compact mechanism was housed on a sturdy one-piece cast aluminum base plate. A tin horn directed sound out the chest of the doll. The motor was usually placed inside a tin container with the winding crank located above the right hip of the doll. Access to the cylinder mandrel was at the back of the doll.

Arthur Patents 1355523 and 1357936 For Improved Phonograph Motor.

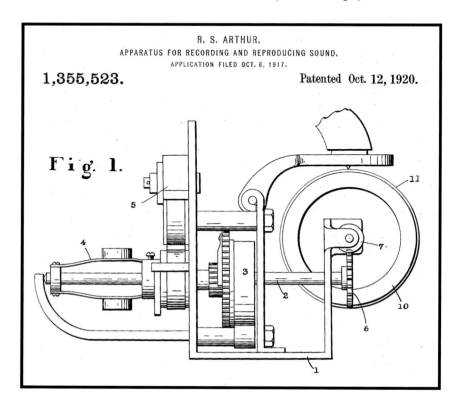

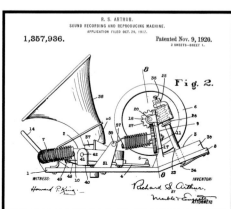

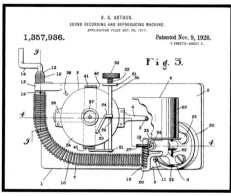

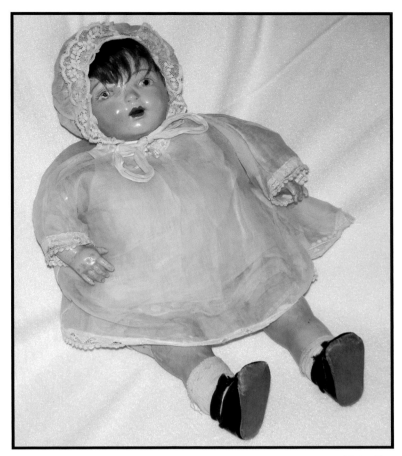

Original Madame Hendren Doll. Bert & Evelyn Gowans Collection. (Value D)

MADAME HENDREN DOLL

Madame Hendren was a trade name copyrighted by the Averill Manufacturing Company. It was 1917 when the name Madame Hendren was given to a doll. The first Madame Hendren, manufactured in 1917, was not a phonograph doll, but a baby doll. It was in 1918 Madame Hendren was marketed as a phonograph doll. The original Madame Hendren phonograph doll was made with composition head, limbs and cloth body. This 22 inch doll was painted a soft ivory with a human hair wig. Her blue eyes were painted. She has an open mouth showing two teeth and her small pink tongue. She is a baby doll that talks by means of the early Arthur motor, which has a small knurled knob to engage the on/off mechanism. Later models use a lever, rather than a knob to turn the record on and off.

Close-up View of Label Found on Madame Hendren Doll Cylinder Packing Box.

AVERILL DOLL TWINS

These twin dolls are a rare delight. They are shown in their original outfits: a pink outfit for the girl and blue outfit for the boy. The fabric is a lightweight cotton material. The baby bonnets are a perfect accent for these twins. These early phonograph dolls measure 21 1/2 inches. The dolls were purchased together as boy and girl twins. They have molded painted hair and painted blue eyes. Their mouths are open showing their two front teeth and a red tongue. The twins have the Averill mechanism and play the celluloid Averill cylinders.

Early Madame Hendren Twin Dolls. Bessie & Floyd Seiter Collection. (Value D)

EARLY AVERILL CYLINDERS AND BOXES

The Original Madame Hendren Doll came with a box of cylinders. They came in sets of six or eight cylinders. The boxes in which the cylinders are packed vary in length. One box is 10 inches long containing five cylinders and another box is 12 inches long, containing eight cylinders. The cylinders are black and found in pink colored boxes. The early cylinders have the song name imprinted on the metal plate and some have a paper label. These cylinders were purchased in a packing box with the Madame Hendren logo pasted on the end of the box and dated "Patented June 11, 1918." Later cylinders are a light blue color.

Box Containing Eight Early Averill Doll Cylinders. Bert & Evelyn Gowans Collection. (Value E)

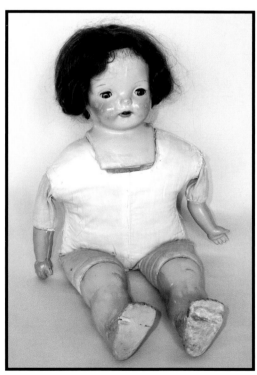

Key Wound Phonograph Doll, 24 Inch. (Value E)

AVERILL PHONOGRAPH DOLL VARIATIONS

There are orphan phonograph dolls. These dolls are unmarked and equipped with various forms of the Averill motor. The sizes of the early phonograph dolls vary from 20 1/2 to 24 inches in height. Some of these orphans have a motor with a metal funnel extending from the phonograph to the top of the head. Holes are found on the top of the head to allow the sound to escape. These dolls have an open mouth with two teeth and pink tongue. They have sleep eyes with lashes. The phonograph mechanism is key wound from the back. A metal cover slides down to cover the motor. On the cover is imprinted, "patented." There is a hole in the center to expose the pin on which the key is placed to wind the motor.

Early Averill Cylinder and Boxes.
Robin & Joan Rolfs Collection. (Value G)

These orphan phonograph dolls play cylinders that are open at both ends. One end of the cylinder is marked with a dark red dye. The center core is cardboard and the outside is celluloid that ranges in hue from dark navy blue to black. Cylinders measure 2 3/16 inches in diameter and 1 1/4 inches in length. The record number is etched on the blank playing surface of the cylinder. Original boxes for the cylinders came with instructions printed on them. The instructions state, "When putting on record, place the red end down." Nursery rhymes and children songs were titles found recorded on the cylinders. A series of doll records were available for children to play on their phonograph doll. Known titles are as follows:

No. 72 Jack and Jill
No. 73 Twinkle, Twinkle Little Star
No. 74 Now I Lay Me Down to Sleep
No. 77 My Dolly
No. 78 Rock-a-Bye Baby
No. 79 Mary Had a Little Lamb
No. 80 Good Morning Merry Sunshine

Key Wound Phonograph Doll, 20 1/2 Inch.
Robin & Joan Rolfs Collection. (Value E)

Early 20 1/2 Inch Madame Hendren Doll.
Robin & Joan Rolfs Collection. (Value E)

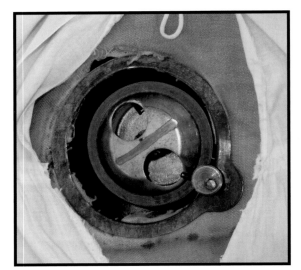

Early Averill Motor With Knob. Patent 1357936 Nov.9, 1920.

Other variations of the early phonograph orphan dolls had a version of the Averill motor with a knob rather than a lever used to start and stop the mechanism. They used a crank that projected from the right side of the doll. These early versions played the Averill blue celluloid cylinders that have a metal insert to facilitate the placement of the cylinder onto the doll motor. These dolls vary in size and facial expressions. They have sleep eyes, an open mouth with two front teeth and human hair wigs in blond, brown and red colorations.

MADAME HENDREN TOKENS

Children who were lucky enough to have a Madame Hendren doll also received a good luck token. Each doll wore this lucky token. It stated: "Madame Hendren Talking and Walking Doll" and had a picture of the doll trademark. There are three variations of this coin. The largest token is 1 1/4 inch in diameter with a walking doll logo on the front. A second smaller coin is 1 inch in diameter and is identical to the larger Madame Hendren token. The third coin is also 1 inch in diameter, has a different doll trademark and states "Madame Hendren Dolls Everybody Loves Them." All three coins have a good luck swastika symbol on the reverse side with the words: "Keep This Coin And Good Luck Will Follow You, Good Luck."

Brass Madame Hendren Tokens. (Value I)

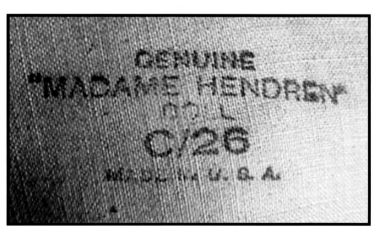

Madame Hendren Doll, Original Yellow Dress, Shoes and Headband.
Robin & Joan Rolfs Collection. (Value E)

Genuine "Madame Hendren" Rubber Stamp Marking Found
on Madame Hendren Doll Body.

DOLLY - REKORD
"Genuine Madame Hendren"

Dolly-Rekord was born in 1922. She weighed five pounds and was 25 inches tall. The Averill Manufacturing Company made this phonograph doll they called Dolly-Rekord. Many phonograph collectors sometimes refer to Dolly-Rekord as the Madame Hendren doll. She has a composition head and limbs with a cloth body. Her hair is either a human hair or mohair wig of various shades of brown, blond, auburn and black. Madame Hendren has an open mouth which shows her little pink tongue and two front teeth. Her painted eyebrows and eyelashes highlight her eyes, which open and close. Her eyes can be brown or blue. She is marked on her cloth body with a rubber stamp stating: "Genuine 'Madame Hendren' Doll, (number) Made in U.S.A." Madame Hendren has a wardrobe of fine delicate dresses in pink, white, blue and yellow. The fabric is a very fine cotton organdy. Valenciennes lace trim of 1 1/4 inch width is found around the hem, sleeves and on two bands down the front of the dress. Another band of daisy or rosebud trim accents the lace around the sleeves and down the front banding. She also has a second dress in her wardrobe that is simpler. This dress does not have the lace down the front of the dress or the daisy or rosebud trim accents. It has bands of lace at the hemline and sleeves. Her socks are a knitted synthetic blend found in white or with four bands of color on the cuff. The bands of color coordinate with the color of the dress.

The phonograph mechanism is different in this doll than in the former dolls. It is accessed from the back of the doll and has no lid that pulls down over the motor. There is a crank that protrudes out of the right side of the doll to wind the motor. A patent number (1357936) found on the base plate for this doll motor corresponds to the improved Averill motor. The horn that carries the sound terminates in the chest of the doll.

Madame Hendren has chubby feet and is fitted with size number two shoes that have one strap with a button closure. The shoe is an oilcloth material with a cardboard type material utilized for the sole. Modern size three baby shoes seem to fit her chubby feet today. Madame Hendren's undergarment is a bit unique as it allows access to the motor and crank. It is a one piece colored panty combination undergarment with a back flap. Elastic gathers the undergarment at the legs. The fabric for the undergarment is lightweight cotton. Madame Hendren was indeed a doll of the 1920s as she enjoyed the flapper look with a silk ribbon worn around her head. She also had the 1920s bobbed curled hairstyle.

Madame Hendren Doll in Second Style Original Dress. (Value E)

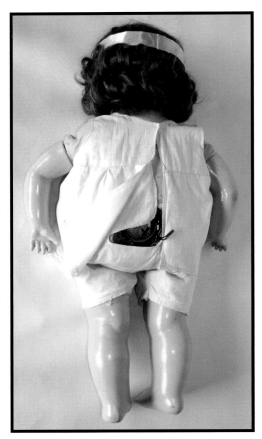

Madame Hendren Doll Undergarment With Flap to Gain Access to Doll Motor.

Many Madame Hendren dolls were not sold in stores. They were given as premiums for selling products or gaining subscriptions to newspapers or magazines. In the ad for this doll, children are enticed to give a few hours of their time and then they can "come and pick out the one you want." Madame Hendren was advertised as the marvelous singing doll that is almost human. The "Doll Lady" stated in the ad in the Tampa Morning Tribune, Tampa, Florida that she wanted children to have the most wonderful and accomplished doll girl in the world. *"She actually sings and prays at night or any time you want her to and she recites before anyone--she is not bashful but modest. She is large as a real live baby and a truly marvelous 'character doll'. Hold her hand and she will walk along beside you singing as she goes. Then the last thing at night, her eyes closed tight, she says her prayers and forgets all her cares. Yes, even the grownups say, 'she's marvelous,' and want one too."*

The Averill Manufacturing Company made the doll until 1925 when production ceased and the EFFanBEE Co. was granted rights to the phonograph doll.

Averill Doll Cylinder With Box. (Value G)

DOLL CYLINDERS

Madame Hendren was quite verbal. She had many cylinders that made her talk and sing. The cylinders are light blue celluloid over a cardboard core. They are 2 3/16 inches in diameter and 1 1/4 inches in length covered on one end with a metal plate with two round finger holes to facilitate removal of the cylinder. The cylinders are identified with various markings such as: Averill Manufacturing Co., New York City, U.S.A.; Universal Talking Toys Co. Newark N.J. U.S.A.; The Mae Starr Dolly; a paper label with the song title and number and some have no markings. It is believed that they may have been manufactured by the Indestructible Record Company of Albany, New York although a reference also cited the Universal Talking Toys Co. A fire destroyed the Albany plant in October of 1922. The source of cylinder records after this date is unknown.

Each Madame Hendren Doll was sold with six cylinders. The titles of these six cylinders are as follows:

> Little Boy Blue
> Now I Lay Me Down to Sleep
> Little Miss Muffet
> London Bridge
> Rock-A-Bye Baby
> One, Two, Buckle Your Shoe

In addition to the six cylinders that came with the doll, additional titles were available. Listed below are titles of doll cylinders we know to exist. There may be many more for this Madame Hendren Doll to talk, sing, or recite.

> Lazy Mary
> Rocking Horse
> Little Bo-Peep
> Mary Had a Little Lamb
> Pussy Cat
> Hey Diddle Diddle
> Twinkle Twinkle Little Star
> Little Girl With a Curl
> Ding Dong Bell
> Humpty Dumpty
> Little Jack Horner
> Bed in Summer
> Bye Baby Bunting
> Ride a Cock Horse
> Old Mother Hubbard

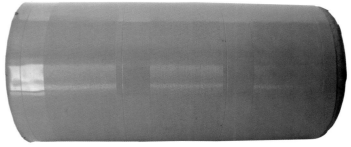

Rare Artifact of Uncut Doll Cylinder. One, Two, Buckle Your Shoe. (Value F)

The songs were recorded on a cylinder measuring 4 1/2 inches long. Three songs of the same title were recorded on one cylinder. The cylinder was cut apart and the metal end cap added and name printed on the metal cap or rim of the cylinder.

Averill Doll Cylinder Without Box. (Value H)

In a brochure for the "Madame Hendren" Dolly-Rekord Doll it states she is "The Educational Doll." Educational cylinder records were also available and these are the cylinders we know to exist:

Adding (1+1=2, 2+2=4, to 9+9=18, 10+10=20)
A Week of Birthdays (Starts with Monday and ends with Sunday)
Counting (1 to 20)
Cat and Dad (Spelling)
Had Fun (Spelling)
ABC
The Two Tables (1x2=2, 2x2=4 3x2=6 to 9x2=18, 10x2=20)

INSTRUCTIONS
HOW TO OPERATE.

1st—Be sure that motor is turned off by turning button on back of doll to right. Push in slightly while turning.

2nd—Push record on cylinder as far as as it will go.

3rd—Wind crank at side of doll as tight as possible.

4th—Release motor by turning button at back of doll to left.

5th—When record has been played, turn button to right again—this stops motor and allows record to be removed.

"MADAME HENDREN"
DOLLY-REKORD

Patented — SINGS RECITES WALKS — Trade-Mark Reg.

THE EDUCATIONAL DOLL

INSTRUCTIONS FOR OPERATING ON BACK

LIST OF RECORDS FOR DOLLY-REKORD" DOLL

Little Boy Blue (No. 21)

Little Boy Blue, come blow your horn!
  The sheep's in the meadow, The Cow's in the corn.
Where's the little boy who looks after the sheep?
He's under the haystack, fast asleep.
Will you wake him? No, not I,
  For if I should he will surely cry.

Prayer (No. 22)

Now I lay me down to sleep.
  I pray the Lord my soul to keep;
If I should die before I wake,
  I pray the Lord my soul to take.
God bless papa, God bless mamma,
  God bless everybody and make me a good girl.
                                        Amen.

Little Miss Muffet No. (23)

There was a little girl who wore a little hood
  And a curl down the middle of her forehead.
And when she was good she was very, very good
  And when she was bad she was horrid!
Little Miss Muffet sat on a tuffet
  Eating of curds and whey,
There came a big spider and sat down beside her
  And frightened Miss Muffet away.

Song: London Bridge (No. 31)

London Bridge is falling down, falling down.
                              falling down,
  London Bridge is falling down, my fair lady.
How shall we build it up again, up again, up again,
  How shall we build it up again, my fair lady.
We'll build it up with silver and gold,
                silver and gold, silver and gold,
We'll build it up with silver and gold, my fair lady.

Song: Rock-A-Bye Baby (No. 32)

Rock-a-bye baby upon the tree top,
  When the wind blows the cradle will rock,
When the bough breaks the cradle will fall.
  And down will come cradle, baby and all.

One, Two, Buckle Your Shoe (No. 33)

One, two, buckle your shoe;
  Three, four, open the door;
Five, six, pick up sticks;
  Seven, eight, lay them straight;
Nine, ten, a good fat hen!
  One, two, three, four, five, six,
Seven, eight, nine, ten.

INSTRUCTIONS FOR OPERATING ON BACK

INSTRUCTIONS FOR OPERATING ON BACK

Averill Reproducer Showing Stylus.

Note Incorrect Patent Number Stamped in Casting. Correct Numbers For Arthur Patents are (1355523) and (1357936).

Averill Reproducer
Top View.

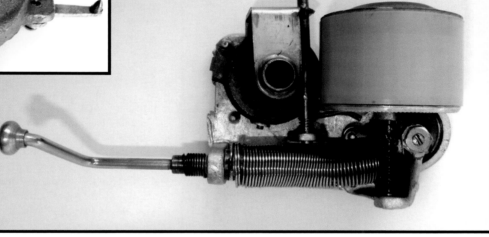

Averill Motor Used in Madame Hendren, Mae Starr and Later Phonograph Dolls.

Averill Tin Plate Housing & Horn.

The Averill cylinder mechanism is housed in a well-constructed tin plate housing. The sound is directed out the front chest of the doll with access to the cylinder mechanism at the back. A small lever starts the motor and positions stylus on the beginning of the record. A crank is utilized to wind the mechanism.

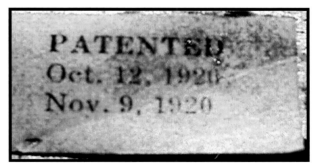

Patent Date Found on Label of Averill Motor.

EFFANBEE DOLL

This 29 inch talking doll has the smoothest skin. That is because she is made by the EFFanBEE Company, which is famous for their "satin smooth" finish. This doll was dipped in a mixture of pigment rather than hand painted. Hand painted details were still added to the lips and eyebrows. She has real eyelashes. Her friend the "Madame Hendren Doll" has painted eyelashes.

Her makers were Bernard E. Fleischaker of Louisville, Kentucky and Hugo Baum who came to America from Germany and were the founders of the famous trademark "EFFanBEE." This may seem like an odd name but they decided upon the name EFFanBEE: EFF (for Fleischaker) and BEE (for Baum). They invented an automatic eye cutting device for making sleeping-eyes for the dolls. This made the business more profitable and efficient. Fleischaker and Baum were granted the manufacturing rights to the EFFanBEE phonograph doll in 1925. The manufacture of this doll commenced between 1925 and 1928.

EFFanBEE Doll With Original Bonnet.
John & Carole Mehling Collection.

EFFanBEE Doll in Original Dress.
Robin & Joan Rolfs Collection. (Value E)

There are conflicting dates on the beginning of the manufacture of the EFFanBEE phonograph dolls. Workers from the Averill Company transferred to the EFFanBEE Company and brought their expertise to the EFFanBEE phonograph doll enterprise. Miss Anna Edele, a well-known doll maker, was hired to make samples and to dress the dolls.

The EFFanBEE doll has a composition stationary head, shoulder and limbs. The dolls are marked "EFFANBEE" on the back shoulder plate of the doll. The body is stuffed with kapok cotton type material. She has an open mouth with four teeth and her eyes open and close. Her dress is similar to the Genuine Madame Hendren doll with less detail. If she were a real little girl, her dress would be a size three. Her undergarment with a flap to expose the motor varies; some undergarments are gathered at the leg, while other styles have a band of material at the legs that coordinates with her dress. She originally wore a beautiful ruffled bonnet that is original to this EFFanBEE doll. Her shoes have one button with a faux buckle found on the front of her more stylish shoes. She has chubby feet and wears a size three baby shoe.

The Averill motor (patent 1357936) is found within her body. A crank projects from the right side of her body. The blue Averill cylinders with the metal end help her recite and sing. The cylinders are marked "Averill Manufacturing Co. New York City, U.S.A." Dolls marked with "EFFANBEE" are fewer in number than the Mae Starr or Madame Hendren dolls. She is distinguished not only by her marking but her beautiful finish and softer hair. The EFFanBEE Company was one of the major doll manufacturers of the late 1920s and 1930s and the trademark is still found on dolls made for children today.

MAE STARR DOLL

Mae Starr is a tall 29 inch doll. She is four inches larger than the Genuine Madame Hendren. Many speculate that she is named after a designer who was connected with the creation of the Madame Hendren doll from the Averill Company. The Mae Starr doll was made from 1928 through 1944, when doll production stopped because of the shortage of materials due to World War II. Mae Starr has a composition head, hands and feet with a cloth body. On the back of the shoulder plate is the identifying name: "Mae Starr Doll." She has beautiful sleep eyes with real eyelashes. The wig is human hair and may be blond or brunette. Her dress is lightweight dotted Swiss cotton. Delicate one half inch lace bands accent the hem of the dress. Mae Starr's undergarment is constructed the same as Genuine Madame Hendren's undergarment with the exception of a 1 3/4 inch coordinating band of dotted Swiss cotton fabric found at the bottom of the undergarment that coordinates beautifully with her dress. Mae Starr's shoes are more stylish with a jewel trim buckle on the front of her size two shoes.

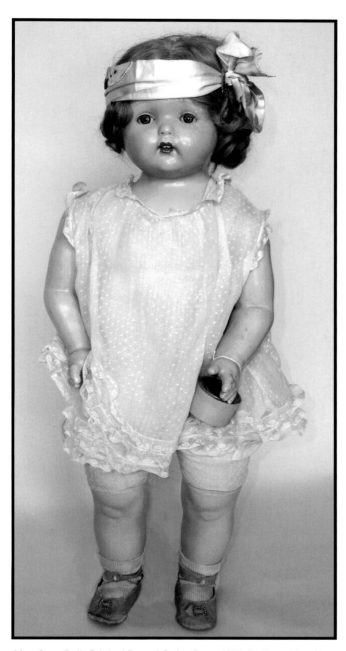

Mae Starr Doll, Original Dotted Swiss Dress With Ruffles. Note Her Shoes With Faux Decorative Buckles. (Value E)

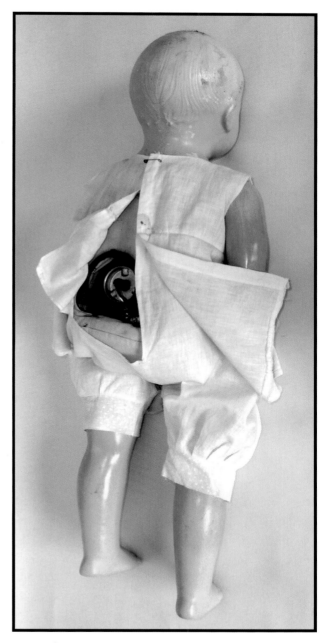

Mae Starr Undergarment Showing Flap & Band of Dotted Swiss Fabric That Coordinates With Her Dress.

Mae Starr Doll Logo Found on Back Shoulder.

Mae Starr utilizes the same Averill motor used in previous models. The motor is found within the body of the doll and the crank projects from the right side of the doll above the hip area. She plays the newer light blue cylinders with the metal end. There is a rare advertising cylinder for Mae Starr titled *The Mae Star Dolly*, which carries the title *The Mae Star Dolly* on the rim of the cylinder. Not to be confused with the "The Mae Star Dolly" imprinted on the metal end caps of some cylinders. Mae Starr recites: *"Hello boys and girls! I'm a Mae Starr Dolly and I can speak and sing for you. And oh, I can spell, too! D-O-G spells woof... C-A-T spells meow... B-I-R-D spells tweet-tweet..."* The cylinders played by the Mae Starr are the same cylinders and songs that are played by the Madame Hendren doll. These cylinders were supplied by the Averill Company. Some cylinders are marked Averill, The Mae Starr Dolly, while others are not marked. The cylinders sold for thirty-five cents each.

These dolls were given as subscription premiums by various large newspaper publishers throughout the United States such as *The Philadelphia Ledger*. They were also sold in retail stores such as Carson, Pirie, Scott & Co. department store at the cost of $20.00 - $25.00. Mae Starr was a very expensive playmate. A novelty doll that talked, sang and with a little help from a child could walk. Mae Starr was not as popular as Madame Hendren, perhaps because of the lack of marketing and fewer dolls manufactured.

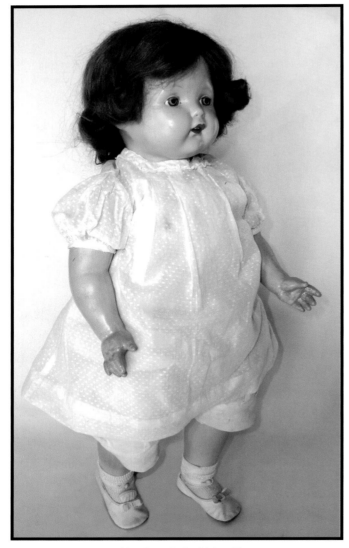
Mae Starr Doll. (Value E)

The Mae Star Dolly Cylinder.
William Kelm Collection. (Value G)

LOVUMS DOLL

"EFFanBEE Lovums" is another trade name under the Fleischaker and Baum firm. These dolls were made in several styles, sizes, shapes, dress styles and gender. Lovums dolls were made from 1928 to 1939. They have a composition head, arms and legs with a cloth body. Their sleep eyes have real lashes. On the shoulder plate is a mark: "EFFANBEE LOVUMS." All Lovums dolls have a loving facial expression that no child or parent could resist. Some have human hair wigs and others have molded hair. They all have the same marking on the back shoulder plate and they are all lovable.

EFFanBEE Doll Pin. (Value I)

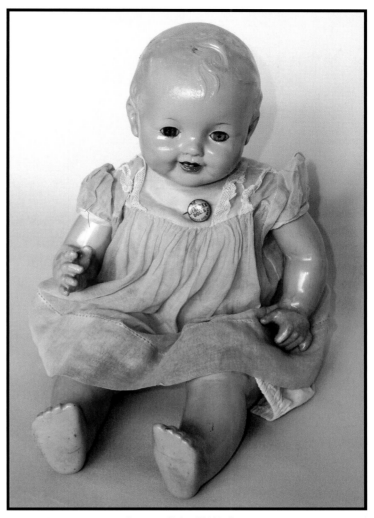

Lovums Baby Girl Doll.
Robin & Joan Rolfs Collection. (Value E)

These cute dolls have a very expressive baby face, with chubby cheeks. The facial expressions are varied, baby like and lovely as the Lovums name conveys. They also have more teeth than other phonograph dolls. They have two upper and two lower pearly white teeth showing through their smile. These dolls vary in height from 19 to 29 inches. The dresses vary with each doll. There is no one dress style for the Lovums dolls. The Averill motor is found in these dolls and they play the blue Averill cylinders. One Lovums doll is known as "Talking Tousle Head." She is distinctive with very curly short hair, known as a caracul wig. A locket can be found around the wrist of a Lovums doll. However, many times these lockets were lost. The locket is heart shaped and states "EFFANBEE DOLLS." Some dolls also wore a colorful EFFanBEE pin with a bird motif that stated: "EFFanBEE DOLLS FINEST AND BEST."

EFFanBEE Logo on Back Shoulder of Lovums Doll.

AMORITA DANCING DOLL

Amorita was the "Pride of the Harem." A dancing doll made by the Dancing Doll Company of 115 East 18th St., New York City, she shimmied on the top of your phonograph. As the ad stated, Amorita shimmies and shakes her hips at the same time, and never gets out of order. She wore a hula style skirt, blue top and beads that moved as she danced her belly dance atop the phonograph to the delight of fathers and their children. This doll came in 9 inch and 13 inch sizes at the price of $2.50 and $3.50 respectively.

Amorita Dancing Doll in Original Box. Lawrence A. Schlick Collection. (Value E)

The Response to Our First Advertisement in this Paper Was So Tremendous that We Have Actually Been Carried Off Our Feet

The result is that we are going to give you the benefit of our vast experience in these lines and give you fair warning that **YOU PLACE YOUR STOCK ORDERS NOW** if you want to get AMORITA in your warerooms for the Holiday Trade.

Amorita shimmies and shakes her hips at the same time and never gets out of order. Amorita is a doll and the mechanism is not visible

Amorita is made in 9-inch and 13-inch sizes and retails for $2.50 and $3.50 respectively. Write your nearest jobber or direct to us

DANCING DOLL CO., INC.

115 E. 18th St.   Phone: 2293 } 9055 } Stuyvesant   **New York City**

THE PHONOGRAPH PHOLLIES

The phonograph was the center of entertainment and phonograph toys were an added accessory to the phonograph that entertained the entire family. It was like going to the movies. The Phonograph Phollies made by the National Company of Boston, Mass. were marketed in the 1920s and as late as 1935. The Phollies sold for $1.00 for two figurines, one a Comedian that looked a great deal like the real comedian of the day "Charlie Chaplin" and the other a Dancing Girl. Another set that sold for $1.00 was a Policeman and Clown. For $1.65 one could have a complete set of five figures called the special combination consisting of the Comedian, Dancing Girl, Policeman, Clown and a

Rube that could also pass as "Uncle Josh." To enjoy this toy you put on a lively record. A heavy driving disc with three rubber feet is placed over the spindle and rests on the record label. A double spring wire is inserted under the thumbscrew on the upper side of the cam and opposite the weighted support foot. Two Phollies figures are attached to the wires and when the record is played, the Phollies begin their antics.

The Phonograph Phollies. Set of 5 in the Original Box. Howard Hazelcorn Collection. (Value E)

PHONO MOVIES

It was billed as "The Funniest Show on Record." The Scarecrow, the Clown and Shuffling Sambo would dance to the lively rhythm of the phonograph. Patented by Dodson and Pelstring, the mechanism would later evolve into the colorful characters and vivid backdrop stage of the Phono-Vaudettes. This lively toy was manufactured by Commercial Art, Fort Thomas, Kentucky. The toy was advertised in the 1921 *Talking Machine World* and retailed for ninety eight cents. When placed on the front edge of the rotating turntable, dancers would shuffle back and forth on the rocking platform, kicking up their heels and dancing to the rhythms of the phonograph record.

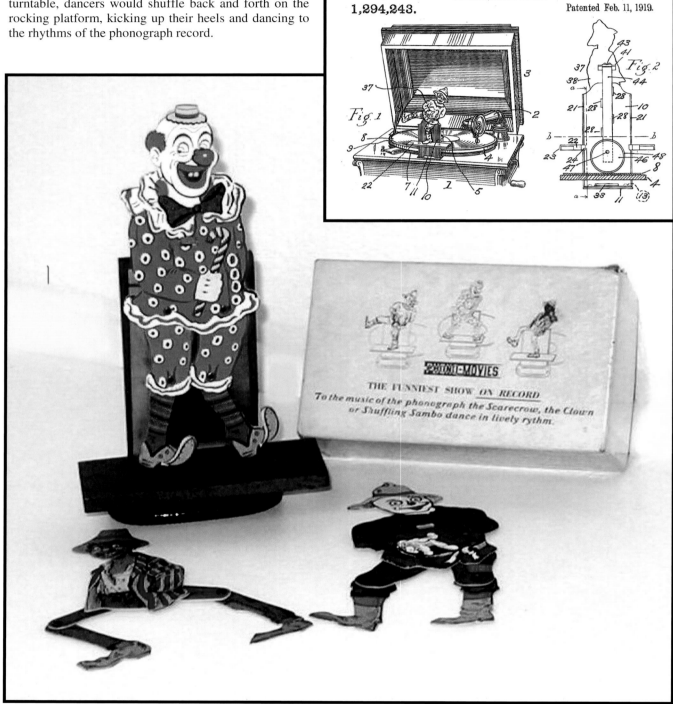

Phono Movies. Howard Hazelcorn Collection. (Value E)

PHONO-VAUDETTES

Phono-Vaudettes Stage and Figures. (Value E)

If The Phonograph Phollies and Phono Movies did not provide the full entertainment for your family you could consider a 1923 phonograph toy, the "Phono-Vaudettes." An evolution of the Dodson/Pelstring patent, this delightful toy with brilliant artwork was manufactured in Covington, KY and priced at $3.50. This toy consisted of a full stage to be placed on your Edison, Victor or any disc phonograph and the performing figures would dance for you. The stage is 14 3/8 inches high and 13 inches wide. The performers are 6 inches tall. There is Shuffling Sambo, a star minstrel. He is happy to dance to the tune of any lively record. Hawaiian Dancer puts into action her native music and trips lightly through a performance that holds the eye in rapt attention. The Scotch Lassie is a nimble girl in kilts and is eager to dance exuberantly at the first note of a bagpipe. Tramp comedian is comical and dances in a droll way to whatever music is furnished him. With imagination and skill families could enjoy Vaudeville shows in the comfort of their own home.

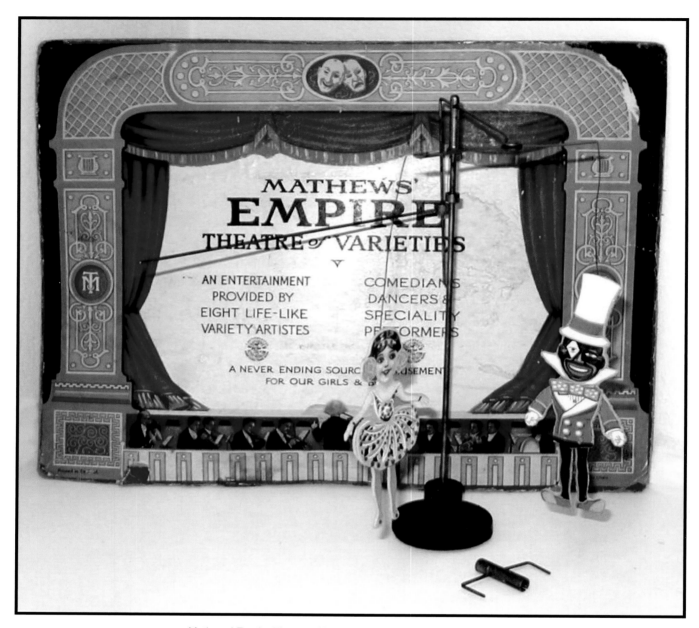

Mathews' Empire Theatre. Howard Hazelcorn Collection. (Value E)

MATHEWS' EMPIRE THEATRE

The British set the stage for your amusement at the Mathews' Empire Theatre. Made at Short St. Leicester, England this decorative stage was set for entertaining the entire family. They stated: "A never ending source of amusement for our girls and boys." Eight life-like variety artists of comedians, dancers and specialty performers provided entertainment. They twirled, danced, and performed from a metal rod extended above the spindle of the turntable. Two or more performers could be on stage at one time as shown on the Mathews' Empire stage. It was a theatre of variety shows to add enjoyment to their favorite phonograph records and bring them alive. The stage is cardboard, lithographed in bright colors with the band members shown below in the orchestra pit.

EDISON-BELL PICTUREGRAM

Let the movies begin on this Edison-Bell Picturegram gramophone of the 1930s. This machine is a spring-driven portable in a leatherette-covered wood case about fourteen inches square. The horn is very small, merely part of the case and does not give very good sound. It plays 78 rpm records that coordinate with the stories. At the edge of the turntable is a pivoted arm bearing a pulley for a belt-drive, which takes the rotation of the turntable to drive a long paper scroll sideways from one roller to another. The scroll and roller are set in a wooden frame at the back of, and just above, the turntable facing the audience.

Edison-Bell Picturegram.
Lawrence A. Schlick Collection. (Value D)

The scroll bears a continuous colored picture illustrating a child's story narrated on an accompanying gramophone disc, and the movie is visible within the square space in the frame. It is truly an amazing picture show! Various spools and records are available. The shellac disc records are seven inches in diameter. The stories are told by Harry Hemsley, a well known B.B.C. radio entertainer. Subjects of the Picturegram show are *Old King Cole, Three Jolly Dogs, Sing a Song of Sixpence, Hey Diddle Diddle, The Three Bears, The Sleeping Beauty, Jack and the Beanstalk, Red Riding Hood, Cinderella* and *Aladdin and The Wonderful Lamp.*

Belknap Circus Wagon. Photo Courtesy of Tim Fabrizo & George F. Paul.
Discovering Antique Phonographs 1877-1929. (Value D)

BELKNAP CIRCUS WAGON

The Belknap circus wagon was patented May 25, 1920. It was made by the Charles H. Belknap Company of Brooklyn, New York. The wagon is made of wood, painted red with a decal scene on the side of the wagon. The band is probably playing the popular circus song *Triumph of the Gladiators*. Instructions for use of this circus phonograph toy are pasted to the underside of the top of the wagon. The instructions suggest purchasing 7 inch children's records such as "Cameo-Kid" and "Playtime." The band members are cardboard, small, fragile and often lost. This phonograph toy had a small acoustic disc talking mechanism, with the sound parading out from the front of the wagon, behind the driver. The circus wagon would move forward as the band played, propelled by the same motor that engaged the phonograph.

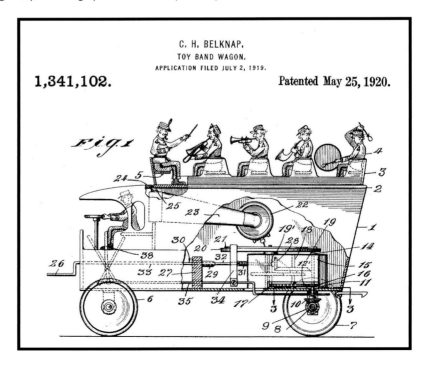

KIDDIE POSTCARDS

Postcards depicting children delighted with their phonographs and records could be sent to friends on holidays, birthdays or any occasion. Postcards were colorful, often comic related and the children made each and every card delightfully cute!

Postcards From the Bob & Wendie Coon Collection and the
John & Frances Wiedey Collection. (Value l Each)

BUBBLE BOOKS

Bubble Book Album. Robin & Joan Rolfs Collection. (Value H)

Bubble Books are the most noted of the early children's records and the first true U.S. series of children's 78 rpm records. They were issued from 1917-1922. Victor Emerson, while working for Columbia, brought together the recording company, Columbia Graphophone; the book publisher, Harper; and artist, Rhoda Chase. Together they created the "Harper-Columbia" Bubble Books that contain three 5 1/2 inch one-sided records. Each book title was a theme that included a written story and verse with colored illustrations along with the record. The editor created the concept of a boy blowing bubbles. In the bubbles he views all the wonderful events that take place in the song. This theme is found throughout the fourteen Bubble Books. In 1924, Victor Talking Machine Company took over the copyright combining two books in one larger 7 inch disc. They reissued six books. Additionally, in 1930, Columbia re-acquired the copyright, with Dodd & Mead as publisher and issued four books #13-16 in the original small format. Each album contained two electrically recorded discs, one single sided and one double sided.

Below is a listing of Bubble Books from 1917-1930:

1917   No. 1 The Bubble Book
        No. 2 Second Bubble Book
        No. 3 Third Bubble Book
1918   No. 4 Animal Bubble Book
        No. 5 Pie Party Bubble Book
1919   No. 6 Pet Bubble Book
        No. 7 Funny Froggy Bubble Book
        No. 8 Happy-Go-Lucky Bubble Book
        No. 9 Merry Midgets Bubble Book
1920   No. 10 Little Mischief Bubble Book
        No. 11 Tippy Toe Bubble Book
        No. 12 Gay Games Bubble Book
        No. 13 Child's Garden of Verses Bubble Book
        No. 14 Chimney Corner Bubble Book
1930   No. 15 Robin and Wren Bubble Book
        No. 16 Higglety-Pigglety Bubble Book

BUBBLE BOOK CUT-OUTS

A cut-out book was advertised at the end of some Bubble Books numbers 13 and 14. The cut-out book was titled *Mother Goose Cut-Outs*. The paper doll cut-out coordinated with the Bubble Book song titles. Children could make these cut-outs dance to the music of their own songs found in the Bubble Books. The cut-outs would be pasted together to look like real people from all sides. A cardboard stand enabled them to stand up by themselves. The child could make a tiny platform for them and place them in the center of the Bubble Book record. As the record played the Bubble Book friends would go around and around, just as though they were dancing. The cut-out book is one of the rarer collectibles associated with the Bubble Books.

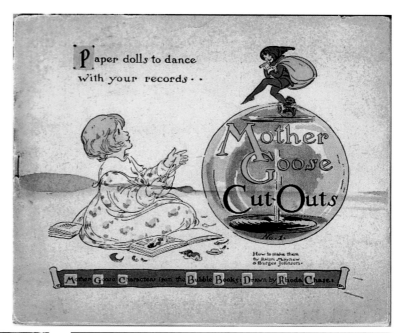

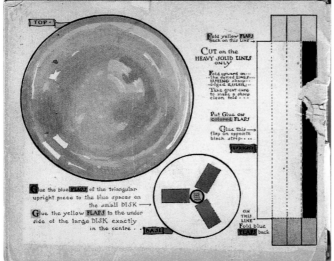
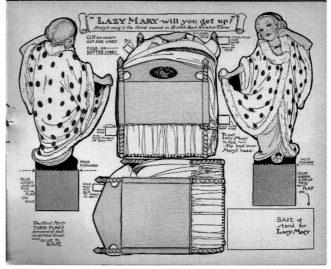

Bubble Book Mother Goose Cut-Out Book and Pages Showing Cut-Outs. Merle Sprinzen Collection. (Value G)

Bubble Books were known as the books that sing. They brought pictures, verses, melody, art, and poetry together in one book. *Little Bo-Peep, Mary and her Little Lamb, Floppy Fly and the Bumble-Bee,* and all the Mother Goose characters were found in picture, story, verse and real phonograph records. Bubble Book sales were also stimulated by child actors hired to participate in organized Bubble Book parties. These parties were noted to draw large numbers of children. The Bubble Books were highly advertised in trade magazines. As one advertisement stated: "Read the stories to the children. Play them on the phonograph. It will keep them quiet and contented for hours. They love the quaint songs and funny verses, and you will love them too."

Illustration of Bubble Book Cut-Out Dancer.

LITTLE WONDER RECORDS

Little Wonder Album. (Value I)   Record Box. (Value F)   Records. (Value I)

Little Wonder Phonograph.
Dick & Jean Zahn Collection. (Value F)

Little Wonder records were made for the enjoyment of adults and children alike. They were a small 5 1/2 inch diameter, single faced record. There are eight label variations for the records with the Little Wonder label. The earliest label is pressed into the shellac of the record. The early paper label records have musical instruments surrounding the center hole of the record. A third paper label design has a happy Little Wonder boy directing the music. It was 1914 when a music publisher, Henry Waterson, manufactured these small records that sold for ten cents each. These records sold in Woolworth's, Kresge's, Sears & Roebuck and other department and music stores. Record albums were sold to store these records and pyro-art record boxes may have been designed to store these Little Wonder records. Early issues of Little Wonder records are quite common and thousands were sold across the nation.

There were two phonographs that were marketed to go with the Little Wonder records. These phonographs were not manufactured by Henry Waterson. One phonograph was called The Little Wonder phonograph and sold for $10.00. It was small, made of cast iron and had an unusual odd looking horn with the tone arm projecting out of the horn. The sound was actually reflected from the back of the tone arm. This phonograph could play lateral or vertical-cut discs.

The little baby record display shown on the left may have displayed Little Wonder or any other record label of a small size. This baby display would be appropriate to display the records and promote another small phonograph called the "Baby." This phonograph has a small internal horn. It was marketed to the public in late 1915. It was advertised to play: "Three full Little Wonder records with one winding." The name of this phonograph originated with phonograph supply manufacturer Otto Heineman of Ohio.

The Little Wonder records played for one-and-a-half minutes each. The public could select from all types of musical selections. These records may have been small, but many were recorded for the pleasure of the adults. Popular hits, bands, marches, fox trots, and even jazz were found recorded on Little Wonder records. Celebrity artists were not often found on these little records. One exception is the song *Back to the Carolina You Love* recorded by the famous Al Jolson on Little Wonder record no. 20. In 1923 Little Wonder records were discontinued. Columbia continued to press the 5 1/2 inch records for the famous Harper-Columbia "Bubble Books for Children."

Baby Record Display. Gfell Family Collection. (Value E)

Small Version of the Baby Phonograph.
Ron & Janet Keuler Collection. (Value F)

Baby Phonograph.
John & Frances Wiedey Collection. (Value F)

KEIMOLA PHONOGRAPH

The Keimola Phonograph was made in Germany in the 1920s. The bright blue horn carried the tunes to the ear of the child. The horn was attached to the reproducer. This small phonograph brought joy to children as they played their favorite records. Beautiful graphics were a highlight of this child's phonograph. The graphics depicted two boys gleefully carrying their phonograph in their toy basket.

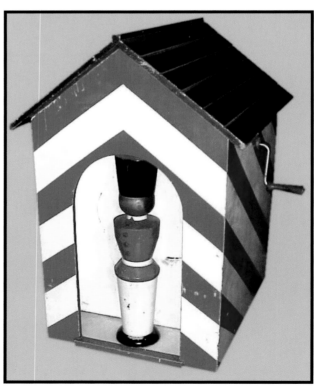

Keimola Child Phonograph.
John & Frances Wiedey Collection. (Value F)

GUARD HOUSE PHONOGRAPH

A lone toy soldier stands guard, protecting his phonograph for the children. As the children open the roof they are surprised to find that this wooden toy soldier was protecting a toy phonograph with their favorite Victor children's record. They can turn the crank and hear the marching band as they imagine the wooden soldier marching to the beat of the drum. The bright red striped guard house phonograph is made by Young Things Phonograph Company, Pasadena, Calif. In the back of the guard house is a door that opens to a storage space for secret treasures.

Guard House Phonograph.
James R. Wilkins, Olden Year Musical Museum Collection.
(Value F)

Bobolink Record Sets No. 2 & No. 4. John & Frances Wiedey Collection. (Value G)

BOBOLINK RECORDS

Children could find two 7 inch Bobolink records in each Bobolink Book. The books were illustrated by Willy Pogany and Maud and Miska Petersham and sold for $1.00 per book. The books were made from 1921-23. Charles Harrison was a featured vocal artist on the first series of Bobolink records. The children could not only be entertained by these children's books, but could play with an Erector set while listening to their favorite songs. The earliest records are credited to A.C. Gilbert Company of Connecticut, manufacturers of the Erector Set, Gilbert Chemistry Sets and other toys of the day. In 1922 A. C. Gilbert sold his record business to his brother, F. W. Gilbert and record labels were redesigned to read "LaVelle Bobolink."

Durium Mother Goose Songs. Lowell Gearhart Collection. (Value H)

DURIUM RECORDS

Children were not forgotten by Durium Products, Inc. For 20 cents, mom and dad could receive a new Durium Hit Of The Week each Thursday at their favorite news stand. Children growing up in the early 1930's could enjoy small 4 inch flexible records such as the *Old King Cole's Party* album. This album contains six thin cardboard laminated records with silhouettes representing the song printed on the back of each record. The children's favorite Mother Goose songs and stories were recorded by Frank Luther.

TALKING BOOK FIGURE RECORDS

The colorful Talking Book records were cut out cardboard figures of popular subjects and animals. A small 4 1/8 inch disc was fastened to the center of the figure. These records were produced by Victor H. Emerson from 1919-1921 and sold for 35 cents by the Talking Book Corporation of NYC. Emerson's patent application called these records a "Phonographic Tablet." The records were riveted to the face side of the card that depicted the song title. On the back of each card a story was told in verse, prose or musical score. Almost half of the talking books are animal figures and the others relate to subjects that would enchant children.

Titles of Talking Book records are as follows in order of matrix numbers:

I Am a Parrot	*The Hip-Po-Pot-A-Mus*	*The Choir Boy*	*Twilight and Dawn In Birdland*
I Am a Lion	*Santa Claus*	*The Elephant*	*The Camel*
The Mocking Bird	*The Tiger*	*Watermelon Coon*	*The Frog*
Mother Goose Talking Book	*The Fox*	*The Tired Baby*	*The Battle of the Marne*
I Am a Dancing Girl	*Christmas Carol*	*The Little Hieland Mon*	*The Victory Book*
I Am Your Uncle Sam			

Talking Book Records. (Value G)

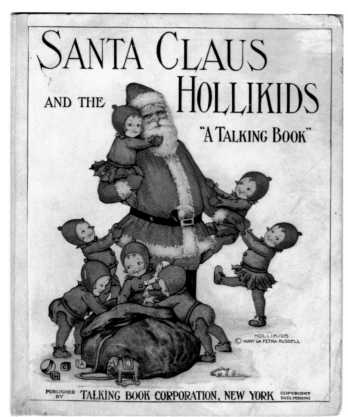

Santa Claus and The Hollikids Talking Book. Robin & Joan Rolfs Collection. (Value G)

TALKING BOOK RECORDS

Talking Book 6 inch discs with the treble clef signature motif label were plain records. Artists brought these records to the attention of their young audience. Mary La Fetra Russell did the pixie and Santa illustrations for *Santa Claus and the Hollikids* talking book and Clara Burd did the illustrations for *The Mother Goose Talking Book.*   Talking Book records were also issued with colorful and artistic paste-on illustrations on the back-side of the record.

Talking Book Records. Lyle Boehland Collection. (Value G)

Kiddie Record Set One. Robin & Joan Rolfs Collection. (Value F)

KIDDIE & PICTORIAL RECORDS

The most beautifully illustrated records are the Kiddie Records. In 1922-1923, the Kiddie Record Co. published two albums made in Plainfield, N.J. and concurrently issued in England. Each album contained six 5 7/8 inch discs. These attractive records are fully illustrated with a color paste-on illustration on one side of the record. The artists Clara Burd and Mr. Helguerd brought the stories to the children by illustrating the nursery rhymes in colorful scenes on the back of the record and in the accompanying story book. They are not picture discs in the truest sense because there are no grooves on the picture side of the disc. An eight volume book, "Mother Goose In Song and Story" with full music score, text and illustrations accompanied each album. They were packaged in a box with a colorful picture record on the front of the Kiddie Record set.

The Pictorial Record is another version of an illustrated children's record. This record has a nursery rhyme pictured on both sides of the record. It is a childproof laminated record.

Pictorial Record. (Value G)

CAROLA PHONOGRAPH

The Carola phonograph was advertised as "The Nightingale of Phonographs." Perhaps because the tone arm is of "Violin Fibre" that prevents a rasping metallic ring, there was no irritating sound as the result of needle scratching. This 22 inch tall phonograph was manufactured by The Carola Company of Cleveland, Ohio. This small phonograph is really not a child's phonograph, but a small phonograph to enchant the adults of the family.

This metal phonograph had a faux mahogany finish. The metal cabinet was made by the Art-Metal Co., Jamestown, NY. The children could have a dignified phonograph for themselves. In an ad for the Carola phonograph they proclaimed: "Music lovers everywhere, whether rich or poor, welcome the Carola as a means of satisfying their music hunger. Its price is sensational when measured by its intrinsic merit--its beauty and its marvelous ability to translate records and to transfuse the voice and spirit of all musicians into the lives of all people. The Carola has so many *exclusive advantages* that your enthusiasm will know no bounds." A few of the advantages of the Carola were as follows: Plays all standard records; Uses any standard needle; Sound waves do not pass through metal; Dust-proof compartment is specially designed to contain records. They boasted that this phonograph will "Make YOUR Family Happy Too!" Of course, if you were not happy at the end of five days, and the Carola was not exactly as represented, the company would return your $15.00.

Carola Phonograph.
John & Frances Wiedey Collection. (Value F)

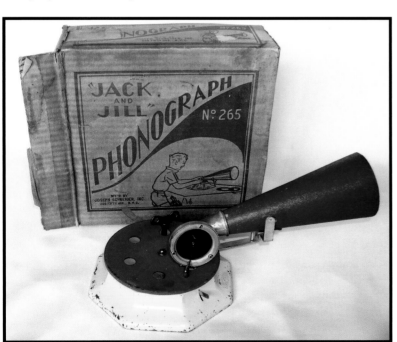

Jack and Jill Phonograph With Original Box.
Robin & Joan Rolfs Collection. (Value F)

JACK AND JILL PHONOGRAPH

Both Jack and Jill can play with this small key wind phonograph. This compact phonograph was manufactured by Joseph Schneider, Inc., 200 Fifth Avenue, New York City. The base and horn of the Jack and Jill phonograph came in various colors. The horn is a cone made of fiber material. The base is a very sturdy metal. This was a very inexpensive and popular children's phonograph. There are no markings on the phonograph or horn. The graphics on the shipping box shows a child playing his favorite records on his new toy, the No. 265 Jack and Jill phonograph.

BING PIGMYPHONES

Bing Pigmyphones in Lithograph Tins. (Value F)

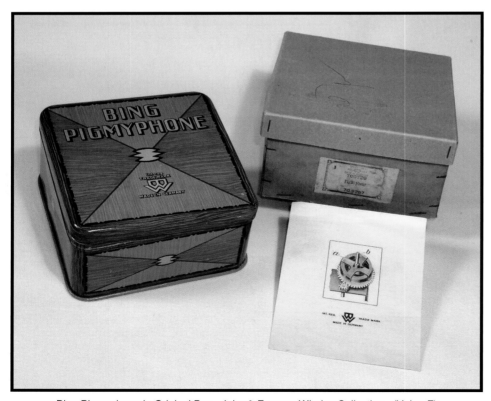

Bing Pigmyphone in Original Box. John & Frances Wiedey Collection. (Value F)

The Bing children's phonograph was hallmarked with the Bingwerke BW trademark. The lithographed tin phonographs were colorfully decorated. Some models had an external horn and the others had an internal horn. The sound boxes have mica or metal diaphragms. The phonographs were introduced to the American market in 1925. Bingola records were also marketed for their phonographs from the years 1926-1929. The Bing Pigmyphone came in different variations. The most popular was the geometric gold design tin box style. The tin box also came decorated with pixies listening to the Bing Pigmyphone. Black singers were also pictured enjoying the music from the Bing phonograph. This style was available in either the green or rust color.

KIDDYPHONE

Kiddyphone was a stage ready to play the kiddie's favorite records. This is a brightly decorated, lithographed tin phonograph with the same horn as found on the Bing Pigmyphones. A Kiddyphone is pictured on the record sleeve for the Bingola Record. Bingola Records were for use with the Bing Pigmyphone, Bing Kiddyphone and Bingola. The Bing Corporation was located on 33 East 17th Street, New York City. The famous Bingwerke BW trademark is found on the side of the phonograph and on the Bingola Record Labels.

Kiddyphone with Original Box. Robin & Joan Rolfs Collection. (Value F)

BINGOPHONE

This Bingophone has a colorful eight-sided tin lithographed case. Another version of this phonograph had a wood grained case. The reproducer is equipped with an aluminum diaphragm and aluminum horn. The phonograph has a key-wind mechanism. The German made Bing phonographs were a popular line of children's phonographs. The Germans were aggressive in marketing tin phonographs for children. The small motors and mass production did not make these toy phonographs the best sounding or most durable. A well-made reproducer did produce good sound to play children's records.

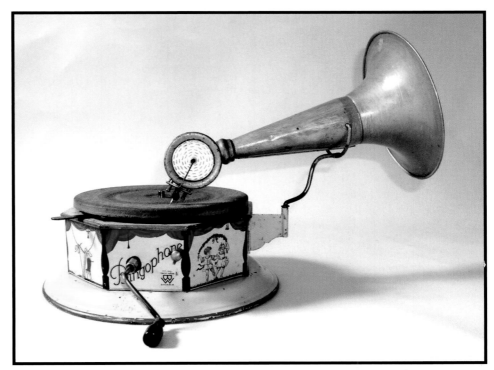

Bingophone with Horn. John & Frances Wiedey Collection. (Value F)

The Bingola II Phonograph.   Bob & Wendie Coon Collection.   (Value F)

BINGOLA II & VALORA PHONO

Bingola I & II, Valora and later children's phonographs made by the German Company Bingwerke were often called "Canned Ham" phonographs because of their shape. Internal horns were found in these models.   The Bingola was highly decorated compared to the German made Valora phonograph.

Valora Phonograph. William Zeeman Collection. (Value G)

Nifty Nirona Phonograph in Original Box. Bob & Wendie Coon Collection. (Value F)

NIRONA TOY PHONO

The Nifty Nirona is one of many toy phonographs by German makers, Nier and Ehmer. The box shows adults dancing to the Nirona, perhaps to market the small phonograph to children and adults alike. The phonograph has a 7 inch turntable. A mica diaphragm and tone arm lead to a shell like reflector horn. The Nifty Nirona shown has black painted scenes of children playing. Scenes on the phonograph varied among nursery rhyme characters, children, and Egyptian motifs. The color and shape of the Nirona also varied with many different models on the market.

Van Toy Phonograph.
Bert & Evelyn Gowans Collection. (Value G)

VAN TOY PHONOGRAPH

A tin horn, a crank and a children's record. That describes this Van Toy phonograph. This toy is made in Cleveland Ohio, by the Van Toy Company. It is a fun toy with a crude tin horn that also serves as the reproducer. The needle attaches to the end of the horn. The fashionable wood base resembles that of a real vintage talking machine. Concealed in the base is the rubber band powered motor! Turning the crank winds the rubber band and this low tech phonograph brings enjoyment to the young listener. The Van Toy decal is adhered proudly to the side of the phonograph. A five inch child's record fits perfectly on the turntable.

Alice in Wonderland 10 Inch Record. (Value F)

RCA PICTURE RECORD

You can have a tea party with the Mad Hatter and Judy Garland. You can meet all the characters from *Alice in Wonderland* on this 10 inch picture record. It was pressed by the RCA Company Inc. of Camden, N.J. in the 1930s.

Winnie The Pooh Record Set. Bob & Wendie Coon Collection. (Value I)

WINNIE THE POOH RECORD SET

"Wherever I am there's always a Pooh" proclaimed the cover of a two record set of Winnie the Pooh by RCA. It was Victor records number 221, 222, 223 & 224 that told the adventures of Winnie the Pooh. "Isn't it funny a bear likes honey" and "I do like a little bit of butter to my bread" are quotes from this wonderful bear that loves his honey and is still as popular today as he was with children of the 1930s.

VICTOR VICTROLA ONE-TWO

In America, the Victor Talking Machine Company made a specially decorated phonograph for children. This phonograph is identical to the Victrola One-One with the exception of the white enamel painted cabinet with colorful decals. It is also known as the Nursery Model. The Victrola One-Two was first announced to the trade on March 31, 1925 and sold for $18.00. It is interesting to note the boy blowing bubbles found on the side of the phonograph is the likeness of the boy found on Bubble Books. In 1924, Victor Talking Machine Company took over the copyright of the Bubble Books. The sound from this phonograph was excellent as it featured a single spring motor, and ten inch turntable. From 1925-1929, 22,673 children's phonographs were shipped to retailers.

Victor Victrola One-Two for Children With Victor Exhibition Reproducer.
Robin & Joan Rolfs Collection. (Value E)

LITTLE TOTS' RECORDS

Little Tots' Albums Showing Record Disc Accompanying the Colored Story Card. Robin & Joan Rolfs Collection. (Value G)

A series of Little Tots' records were issued by Regal Record Co., New York from 1923-1938. Originally sold separately with illustrated sleeves, they were later produced in album sets containing three or four 7 inch two-sided discs. The highlights of these albums are the beautiful "picture and verse cards." Two cards measuring 5 X 6 inches with color illustrations accompany each record. The child could see the picture, recite the verse or story and then hear it reproduced. The artist, Maud Trube, illustrated approximately 78 cards with pictures to inspire the imagination of the children as they were listening to the nursery rhymes on the records. The Little Tots' records originally retailed for 25 cents in individual sleeves and later at $1.00 for each album. The fifteen-year history makes these one of the most successful child's record labels with a catalog featuring 110 selections. Later production was taken over by the American Record Corporation. After 1937, the records continued to be issued under the label of "Playtime Records."

Each album cover was beautifully illustrated with one of Maud Trube's cards. Below is a list of the album titles:

No. 1. Merry Song Book
    2. Happy Day Book
    3. Jolly Game Book
    4. Story Hour Book
    5. Christmas Book

No. 6. Lullaby Book
    7. Patriotic Book
    8. Medley Book
    9. Sunshine Book
   10. Mother Goose Book
   11. The "Dance" Book

PLAYTIME RECORDS

Playtime records were the longest lived 78 rpm children's brand records. They date from 1924 to the 1950s. The 7 inch double sided records were electrically recorded. They sold for 15 cents each or in an album of six for $1.00. For years after 1937, the Little Tots' records were issued under the label "Playtime Records." However, the records were issued without the colorful nursery rhyme cards. These records did have multicolored labels and sold for 15 cents. Later records were pressed in plastic.

Advertisements stated that these records could be played on any toy or adult phonograph. Recordings were popular nursery rhymes, games, jingles, school songs and stories. They were promoted as both fun and educational. There were forty-three different records for the little ones to select from. They were electrically recorded and had a loud sound that children enjoyed. Songs were simple and included sound effects that children could recognize.

YOUNGSTER, CAMEO-KID RECORDS

Children's records could be purchased for 15 cents, 25 cents and $1.00 for an entire album. The Grey Gull Company produced records under the "Youngster" label in the 1920s. These 6 inch records were electrically recorded. The record sleeves were decorated with nursery rhyme characters. On the record children were instructed to change the needle every time the record was played. The Bingola records were also pressed by Grey Gull.

Cameo-Kid records were advertised as: "The Quality Juvenile Record." They sold for 15 cents each and as the record sleeve stated brought "Happy moments for the little ones." Cupids decorated the record sleeve for the Cameo-Kid record. They were produced by the Cameo Record Company.

78 RPM Children's Records. (Value I)

CHILD RECORDS

Jackie Coogan Record Sleeve. (Value I)

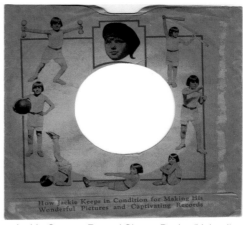

Jackie Coogan Record Sleeve Back. (Value I)

In the summer of 1925 Cameo Record Company signed child star Jackie Coogan to make records. Jackie gained his fame starring as "The Kid" with Charlie Chaplin. The records sold for 20 cents each in record sleeves showing Jackie Coogan in movies and everyday activities.

The Brunswick Company signed up Davey Lee, diminutive protégé of Al Jolson in the films *Singing Fool* and *Say It With Music*.

The 7 inch Kiddie Koncert Karton records were produced for children from 1924-28. The witch was a logo on the record label. This record is made by the American Record Mfg. Co., Mass.

Davey Lee & Kiddie Koncert Record.
Bob & Wendie Coon Collection. (Value I)

Non-breakable records titled Junior Operettas were made by the Vulcan Record Corporation of New York. They were introduced in the August 15, 1922 edition of the *Talking Machine World*. They were made of a semi-flexible black compound laminated over thin cardboard cores. The rendition of *Little Red Riding Hood* used a ten piece band, a quartet, female duet, well known whistler and animal imitators.

Junior Operetta Series Little Red Riding Hood.
Bob & Wendie Coon Collection. (Value G)

"His Master's Voice" Songs for Little People Album. (Value H)

"HIS MASTER'S VOICE" SONGS FOR LITTLE PEOPLE

This wonderful Book No. 1 - Record 216379, contains Songs for Little People. The album was copyrighted in 1933 for the Berliner Gram-O-Phone Company Limited. The book contains the nursery rhymes that children could read while listening to the record.

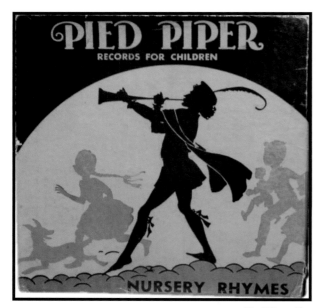 

Pied Piper Record in Box. (Value I)

PIED PIPER & LISTEN LOOK PICTURE BOOK RECORDS

Pied Piper records were from the Catalog of Music You Enjoy, Inc., New York. The records had a yellow label with the Pied Piper leading the children in song. They recorded nursery rhymes, cowboy songs, dances and marches. Pied Piper was the recording label of the Listen Look Picture Books. The sixteen page book gave toddlers color pictures and stories to look at as they listened intently to the stories told. These double-faced records were from the Catalog of Music You Enjoy Inc., New York City. Children could read along as the story was being told on these Listen Look Picture Books of 1941. Parents could get all six Listen Look Picture Books: *Little Red Riding Hood, Cinderella, Myrtle the Turtle, Little Black Sambo, The Three Little Pigs* and *Alice in Wonderland.*

Listen Look Picture Books.
John & Frances Wiedey Collection. (Value I)

Raggedy Ann Sunny Songs Albums. (Value I)

RAGGEDY ANN RECORDS

Music You Enjoy, Inc., New York, manufactured Kiddie Records. They were unbreakable and had a colorful label related to the song title. Nursery rhymes and cowboy songs were on their list of records for children. Raggedy Ann was a favorite doll of little girls. *Raggedy Ann's Songs of Happiness* brought joy to any little girl who loved her Raggedy Ann doll. Victor records had a special three record set with record numbers 227-228-229. The recording artists were Johnny Gruelle and Will Wooden. These Raggedy Ann records were issued in 1932.

Official Boy Scout Record of 1925
Recorded for the Boy Scouts. (Value H)

Raggedy Ann Album. Gfell Family Collection. (Value I)

BOY SCOUT RECORD

The Official Boy Scout Record was issued in 1925. This 10 inch disc featured *Boy Scout Bugle Calls*. The green label had Boy Scouts on the label. This disc was credited to the Cameo Record pressing plant.

DADDY LEW LEHR RECORDS

Daddy Lew tells a story on his 6 inch plastic record. It is an "unbreakable hi-fidelity recording" illustrated by Henri La Mothe. When the bell rings on the record, the attentive little ones could move the picture wheel to bring into view the scene being described in the story. Twelve different story sets include favorite children's tales such as *Cinderella, Little Red Riding Hood, The Ugly Duckling, The Three Little Pigs, The Lion and the Mouse, The Three Bears* and others. Produced in the late 1940s and early 1950s by Shelley Products, the device seemed destined to compete with television for children's attention.

Daddy Lew Record. Lowell Gearhart Collection. (Value I)

Shirley Temple Bluebird Record.
Pickwick 33 1/3 Record & Latest Popular Song Hits Leaflet. (Value I)

SHIRLEY TEMPLE RECORDS

At the age of seven Shirley Temple was rated the number one box office attraction. Her career started in Baby Berlesks. She went on to star in Baby Take a Bow, Bright Eyes, The Little Colonel, Curly Top, The Littlest Rebel and Poor Little Rich Girl to name a few of her popular films. Her songs were hits of the day and every little girl wanted to be Miss Curly Top. Bluebird Kiddie Records issued her popular songs like *Baby Take a Bow, When I Grow Up,* and *On the Good Ship Lollipop* in the mid 1930s. Shirley Temple narrated several stories on 78's and her songs are still being recorded today. The Shirley Temple doll was a popular doll of the day, but did not talk. Shirley Temple's voice is remembered on film, record and sheet music. Her dancing, dimples, curly hair and talent made her the most popular child star in history. Shirley Temple was a doll. She was the most adored child actress of the depression years. Shirley Temple was an original and her records bring us back to the times when we had *Animal Crackers in My Soup.*

2 - 48

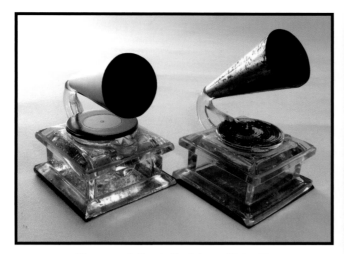

Phonograph Candy Container. (Value F)

CANDY CONTAINER PHONOGRAPH

A little girl is photographed with her favorite ball and a glass phonograph candy container. The base of the phonograph was filled with small candy beads. The phonograph measured 2 3/4 x 5 inches high including the three inch tin horn. The container had a sliding tin bottom so the yummy candy could be removed. A second style phonograph candy container could also serve as an inkwell. It has a removable tin record top to cover the inkwell.

Photograph of Girl with Phonograph Candy Container. (Value I)

TOOTSIE TOY

Almost every girl had a dollhouse. They played mother, wife and decorator. No playhouse was complete without a Victrola. Tootsie Toy, a well known maker of miniature metal toys, made several models of upright Victrolas for the children's playhouse in 1925. The Victrolas came in many colored finishes of black, blue, beige and the Vernis-Martin gold cabinet. The Tootsie Toy Company made a full array of furnishings for the dollhouse.

Tootsie Toy Victrola With Furnishings and Accessories. Kathy Zeeman Collection. (Value H)

PHONO ZOETROPES

The Kinephone was a Gramophone - Cinema. This toy provided the viewers with motion pictures on their phonograph turntable. The toy consisted of a metal rod, center wood block and a slotted disc. Five cardboard discs measuring 7 inches were included with the toy. Each disc has thirteen progressive images in black and white. The disc was placed on the turntable and viewed through the slots of the rotating viewer. An animated character became visible. You could see a figure that resembled the famous tramp, Charlie Chaplin; Felix the Cat; child jumping rope or lady dancer.

Kinephone in Original Box With Discs. Dan Zeeman Collection.   (Value G)

For five cents the family could purchase a movie strip to view on this 4 in 1 Moviescope. The zoetrope would be placed on the turntable and the animated movies began. It was manufactured by G.W. Witte, 1727 Ludlow Street, Philadelphia, Pennsylvania. Two new picture strips were released each week for the enjoyment of the family.

Witte's Moviescope Phonograph Toy. Gfell Family Collection. (Value F)

PHONOGRAPH TALKING PROJECTORS

Mickey Mouse Talkie-Jecktor. John & Frances Wiedey Collection. (Value E)

Talkie-Jecktor Record. (Value I)

Fans of Mickey Mouse could view their favorite cartoon on the Mickey Mouse Talkie-Jecktor of 1929. Records coordinated with the cartoon strips of Mickey's adventures. To the delight of children they could view Mickey at home with their friends. The projector had two lenses that projected alternating images simulating animation. This was no easy matter since the record was placed on the key wind phonograph and as the show began, the child would need to turn the film at a constant rate of speed to coordinate with the record. The joy was seeing Mickey Mouse do his magic to the sound of the recording. The Talkie-Jecktor Record was manufactured by the Movie-Jecktor Co., New York, NY. A 1936 Sears catalog advertised a Mickey Mouse Talkie-Jecktor for $1.98. A set of two 39 inch colored films and one double faced six inch record was forty-two cents. The music on these records was recorded by Irving Berlin.

This talking projector had a belt drive that played both the film and record at the same time. The key was to crank at a steady speed. A fiber horn projected the sounds to the action films. There were several talking projectors made for the amusement of having movies at home. The sound quality was not like the movie theatre and the picture was not large screen quality, but a mere 18 inches wide.

Phonograph Talking Projector. Gfell Family Collection. (Value F)

Ourotone Phonograph Projector. Gfell Family Collection. (Value F)

The Ourotone projector has an unusual dome shaped diaphragm horn. The sound and the paper roll filmstrip were synchronized. No crank is found on this projector. A common 25 watt light bulb was used to project the Duracolor film strip which acted as its own diffuser. Duracolor film strips were available for this combination projector and phonograph from the Durable Toy and Novelty Co., 200 Fifth Ave., New York.

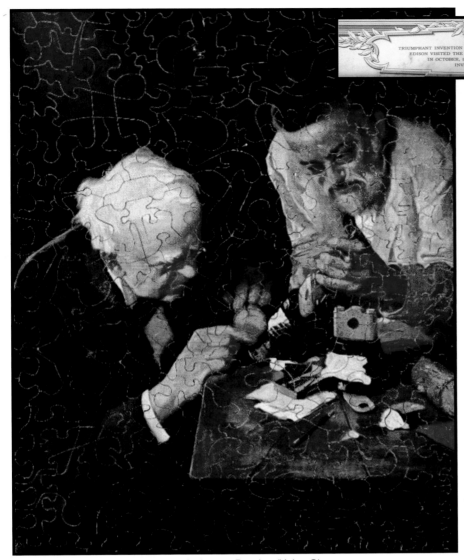

Edison - Steinmetz Puzzle. (Value G)

EDISON AND STEINMETZ PUZZLE

Thomas Edison was great at solving puzzles. This 300 piece puzzle has the great inventor Thomas A. Edison and the brilliant researcher Charles P. Steinmetz comparing notes. This is a picture of the two scientists at the Schenectady research facility in October of 1922. They studied the results of Dr. Steinmetz's investigation of artificial lightning. Triumphant invention and brilliant research were brought together at this historic meeting.

THE QUIZ OF THE WIZ GAME

This 1921 game is divided into three classes, historical and geographical, general, and technical. Players were given three cards with a question. Answer as many questions as you can correctly and you may be as great as Thomas A. Edison, the Wizard of Menlo Park. As the directions exclaim "Mr. Edison's province has been to electrify us." The Quiz of the Wiz is a game for everybody.

The Quiz of the Wiz Game. (Value G)

Victor Victrola Puzzle. (Value G)

Victor Artist Puzzle. (Value G)

PUZZLES

What could be more fun than a puzzle? In 1922 the Victor Company used puzzles to advertise their Victrolas and records. They claimed to be the first to use jigsaw puzzles as advertisements. They were given away to customers and cost the retailer $15.00 per thousand. The puzzles were given to potential customers who filled out cards stating their name, address and musical interests. Dealers also had puzzle contests for children to "Try for a Speed Record" of putting the puzzles together. The children could select from two puzzle styles. They came in envelopes that told the child "You and your family will have lots of fun with the contents of this envelope. You may be able to solve the problem and learn its secret, but how quickly can you do it? Faster than any one else?" One puzzle depicted the Victor artists on a Victrola record titled: *The Names That Everybody Knows, Are in the Victor Catalogue*. The second puzzle is a living room setting with a Victrola and all the Victor artists in miniature size surrounding the Victrola.

"His Master's Voice" Puzzle.
Robin & Joan Rolfs Collection. (Value F)

Nipper and the Gramophone is the famous logo of the RCA Victor Company. Nipper could be found within a puzzle box that bears the likeness of a 1933 REA-84 Victor Electrola. The bottom of the box stated: "Jig Saw Puzzle of the World's Greatest Trade Mark." The puzzle and box were lithographed in the U.S.A. by E. E. Fairchild Corp. NY. The unique aspect of this puzzle is that many of the pieces are in the shape of Nipper and the Gramophone and the letters V I C T O R are also part of this challenging puzzle.

Horserace Turntable Game. Lawrence A. Schlick Collection. (Value F)

GRAMOGAMES Turntable Toy. (Value H)

TURNTABLE RACE GAMES

It's off to the horse races. Set up the horses at the starting gate. Wind up the phonograph. Watch the turntable spin as you bet on your favorite runner. Around and around they race on the turntable until they get to the finish line. It is a game of chance to see whose horse finishes first.

Which Horse Wins Game. Pat Zeeman Collection. (Value H)

The GRAMOGAMES circa 1930-40s were turntable games. Players placed their stake on a board. The disc is placed on the turntable. The turntable is stopped, tone arm is lifted and the needle is rested on the extreme edge of the disc adjacent to the winning section.

The 1947 game of "Which Horse Wins?" was mysterious and exciting for the entire family. The puzzle record played and a different horse won each time. These games were more of an adult gambling game than a child's game. Nevertheless, the whole family could join in the fun.

GENERAL PHONOGRAPH

The General Phonograph M f g . Company of Elyria, Ohio has a fishy history. It was 1917 when Otto Heineman, owner and President of The General Phonograph Company, purchased A.F. Meisselbach & Bro. Co. William and Gus Meisselbach wanted to retire and Gus wanted to spend more time fishing. At this time the Meisselbach Company was producing large quantities of phonograph motors for the General Phonograph Company and other companies. The A.F. Meisselbach Company made fish casting reels from 1922-1928. During that time they produced some very rare casting reels with the brand name "Okeh." In the early 1920s Okeh was the name of the record label owned and manufactured by the General Phonograph Company of New York City. They sold the record label and decided to come out with a new line of fishing reels with the Okeh label.

Baby Cabinet Phonograph 17 1/2 Inches High
With Mother Goose Figures. (Value F)

Otto Heineman came from Germany where he was associated with the Carl Lindstrom Aktien-Gesellschaft Company. He stayed in the U.S. at the outbreak of the war. In the U.S. he contracted with the Garford Mfg. Company to produce high quality phonograph motors. With his expertise the company manufactured toy phonographs to appeal to the youth of the day. They were marketed under trade names of Genola, DeLuxe and Baby Cabinet. Nursery rhyme characters decorated the tin cabinets of these children's phonographs.

Genola, The General Phonograph Co. Elyria, Ohio Decal.

Genola Toy Phonograph Retailed For $5.00 in 1925.
Robin & Joan Rolfs Collection. (Value F)

The General Industries Co. Elyria, Ohio Label.

De Luxe Upright Child's Phonograph.
Gfell Family Collection. (Value E)

Baby - Cabinet Upright Child's Phonograph.
John & Frances Wiedey Collection. (Value E)

By the late teens the lady of the house sought phonographs that were enclosed in upright cabinets. Victrolas were in vogue and set the standard. It seemed that all phonographs ended with an "ola." Children's phonographs also took on the style of the day. They were upright and had room for record storage. They not only came with childlike motifs, but also wood grained and faux mahogany finishes. The ad in the January, 1924 *PLAYTHINGS* magazine exclaimed: "Our Toy Phonographs are real talking machines with splendid sound boxes, strong motors and a tone arm that reproduces clearly and musically. The Baby De Luxe Phonograph is a beautiful piece of furniture for the nursery as well as a good phonograph. The Baby Cabinet is a little sister of the De Luxe models and is very attractive. The Genola is the smallest, practical, portable machine made." Children had to wind the crank and change needles. The General Phonograph Company of Elyria, Ohio kept up with the times and gave the child a phonograph just like mom and dad's Victrola. These children's phonographs retailed from $5.00 to $25.00.

The General Industries Co. 1929 Advertising for The New Genola and New DeLuxe Console Phonograph. (Value I)

Toyola Phonograph. Robin & Joan Rolfs Collection. (Value F)

TOYOLA PHONOGRAPH

This suitcase phonograph for children had a colorful interior. The child could take this phonograph anywhere. The Toyola phonograph was made by the Berg A.T. & S. Co. Inc. of Long Island, New York circa late 1920-30s. A tin horn amplified the sound of the popular children's records of the day. Children were taught to change the needles after playing each record. The needles were called "Twinkle Tips" by the Goldentone Company.

RECORDS 1930s-40s

PLAYSONG Record Co. of New York had production recording artists such as "The Mother Goose Players," "The Wild West Singers" and the "Merry Melody Singers" record songs on their 6 1/2 inch laminated cardboard records.

PICTURtone Records, Inc. of New York had "Treasure Tales" for children like *The Cat and the Fox* and *The Beggar and The Woman Who Pecked*. These 6 1/2 inch records told stories to young children of the 1940s.

Playsong and PICTURtone Records. (Value I)

There were children's records for every occasion like the 6 inch *Happy Birthday* record by Toy Toon Records. The records were unbreakable and inexpensive. Records in the shape of Easter eggs could be found in the Easter egg hunt on Easter morning. These bunny records were made by the Phonographic Records Inc. Woodside, New York. The record label message to children was "A Record from the Easter Bunny."

Easter Bunny & Toy Toon Records.
William Zeeman Collection. (Value I)

Toy Toon Records.
Ben Zeeman Collection. (Value I)

VOCO Circus Record Set. Pat Zeeman Collection. (Value G)

Laugh Phonograph Record. Dan Zeeman Collection. (Value I)

VOCO RECORDS

The VOCO children's records were not only colorful, but were in the shape of the animal or character depicted in song. VOCO made cutout records in the shape of Santa, the Easter Bunny and other fanciful figures in 1948. The "Circus" was the most vivid record set by VOCO. The cardboard envelope that contained the circus show was the tent. There was a Ringmaster, Elephant, Tom Cat the Tightrope Walker and Rover the Strongman.

"Laugh Laugh Phonograph" is a favorite of children and phonograph collectors alike. This song recorded on a VOCO record showed the importance of the phonograph in everyday life. Children's records brought amusement and laughs to every child who owned a toy phonograph.

VOCO Children's Six Inch Records. (Value I)

VOCO Christmas Records. Gfell Family Collection. (Value H)

VOCO started as a greeting card company. From 1946 to 1949, they made two-sided six inch records for children. A recording laminated to the colorful picture on the cardboard core told the story. There were many records children could select from. Records that amused and records that taught, *Don't put things in Your MOUTH!* or *Watch Out! Be Careful!* and *Let Mommy Know Where You Are*, provided moral lessons for children.

Songs of Christmas came in a boxed set. They were to be Christmas gifts to little friends. Each record could be sent to a little friend in an envelope with dear old Santa holding a package label. The record plus the lyrics to the song could be sent out in the mail. The VOCO record company made this set for Christmas 1949. This box of Christmas tunes is still waiting to be sent to some lucky child at Christmas. The colorful records and envelope would bring cheer to any child.

PLAYOLA PHONOGRAPH

"A toy phonograph with a natural life-like tone. Plays just like mom and dad's phonograph." That is what enticed children to convince their parents to buy this miniature phonograph by the Atlas Toy Company of Chicago, Illinois. This 1947 toy was made of the new material called plastic. The small 4 inch records were written and produced especially for the Playola Phonograph. The records came in albums just like the grown-ups had. Each Playola came with Goldentone Needles especially manufactured for children's records. The children were also given a sample record to learn how to turn the crank at the proper speed.

Playola Phonograph With Records in Original Box. Robin & Joan Rolfs Collection. (Value G)

Kitty "Play Phono." Charlie Hummel Collection. (Value G)

KITTY "PLAY PHONO"

This child's phono is the cat's meow. It is a simple hand wind plastic phonograph with a lithographed tin horn. The kitty on the box shows how easy this child's phonograph is to set up and play. This nifty kitty toy phono was made by the Empire Product Co. of Cincinnati, Ohio in 1949.

2 - 63

A TALKING BOOK

In 1941, RCA Talking Book Corp. of America Inc. and Garden City Publishing Company of New York made this unbreakable sound track of "Noah's Ark." Children could look at the pictures twirling on the turntable and listen to the story of Noah's Ark. The animals would go around on the turntable two by two as they were entering Noah's Ark.

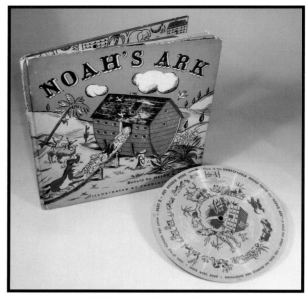

A Talking Book Record, Noah's Ark.
Bob & Wendie Coon Collection. (Value I)

Little Golden Record. Ben Zeeman Collection. (Value I)

LITTLE GOLDEN RECORDS

The "Little Golden Records" were billed as unbreakable! They were copyrighted in 1948 by Simon and Schuster Inc., Rockefeller Center, New York and originated by Sandpiper Press for Golden Records. The Golden Books were the most popular books published for children in the 1940s. The record sleeve was beautifully illustrated and the stories were adapted from the Little Golden Books. The Circus Time record was under the musical direction of Mitch Miller. He was widely known for sing along music and a popular television show of the 1960s. Little Golden Records brought the classics to children with Mozart's Turkish March featured on the record entitled Little Pee Wee. The yellow plastic records were recorded in high fidelity for the best sound of the day.

RCA VICTOR RECORDS

RCA Victor records and Little Nipper promoted records titles such as *Winnie the Pooh, Little Black Sambo,* and *The Little Red Engine That Could,* on their yellow vinyl 45 rpm records. When the readers would hear Little Nipper bark they knew it was time to turn the page of the storybook. A unique Winnie-the-Pooh storybook album could be turned upside-down for another story.

45 RPM Children's Records. Gfell Family Collection. (Value I)

TOONO

Play a game of Toono. In 1946 Adele Girad was "The Toono Lady." The object of the game was to fit four Toono chips vertically or horizontally on the board. The songs suggest the picture on the Toono board such as *London Bridge, Old King Cole, Mary Had a Little Lamb* and other nursery rhymes. It was like a game of Bingo, only to music. Toono was manufactured by Toono Inc. of Hartford, Conn. Three records, Toono boards and chips were included in this musical game.

Toono Musical Game. Bob & Wendie Coon Collection. (Value I)

Superman Records. Bob & Wendie Coon Collection. (Value H)

SUPERMAN RECORDS

"Faster than a speeding bullet. Able to leap a tall building in a single bound. It's a bird. It's a plane. It's..." It was song and adventure in the Magic Ring. The Magic Ring was a 78 rpm record that looked like magic on the turntable as the adventures of Superman were told by the original radio cast. Stories of the Flying Train and Magic Ring came to life as children listened intently to the adventures of their favorite superhero. The records were double sided by Musette Records of Steinway Hall, New York. A 1947 copyright is found on the records.

Record Guild of America Picture-Play Records. The Small 6 1/2 Inch Records. (Value I)   The Larger 10 Inch Records.   (Value G)

A Variety of Record Guild of America Records With Sleeves. (Value I)

RECORD GUILD OF AMERICA RECORDS

These records were made from 1948 to 1951 and vary in size, shape and materials. The most commonly found were the Record Guild of America records made of durable vinyl. The company termed these durable records a "Sealed-Edge Picture Record." The graphics are very clear and colorful. This company also made traditional cardboard records that were packaged in eye catching record sleeves. The records had the seal of approval from *Parents Magazine.* The 10 inch Record Guild records are rarely found. These 10 inch records may be mistaken for those of another company because they have in bright letters, "PICTURE PLAY" on the record. The hues found in these larger records are astounding and the tunes really set one's feet a danc'n'.

PETER PAN GRAMOPHONE

This sturdy little talking machine was no larger than a camera, and as easy to carry. There were many brands of these compact model talking machines on the market. Brand names such as Pet O Fone, Mikiphone, Cameraphone, Excelda, Thorens, were all marketed as compact talking cameraphones. These portable phonographs were mainly for the adult market. They retailed from $12.00 to $25.00. The Peter Pan Gramophone was made by the Marysville Products Company, Marysville, Michigan in 1926.

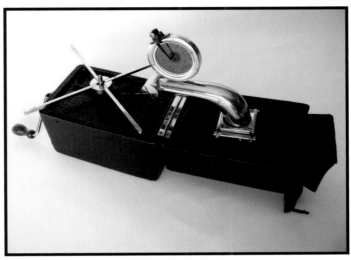

Peter Pan Camera-Phone. (Value F)

GAMA-PHOLA PHONOGRAPH

The German made Gama-Phola was made with different lithographed designs on the tin bases of these inside horn phonographs. The animals and children on these Gama-Phola phonographs tooted their horns as the music played. Made circa 1930-40 they are cheerfully detailed to enchant children to enjoy their 78 rpm records.

EXCELLO PHONOGRAPH

The Excello phonograph was a simple hand wind child's phonograph. It was not colorful, a basic brown color. The cardboard cone horn projected the sound of children's tunes. This phonograph was made by the Excello Talking Machine Company at 31 South Ninth Street, Philadelphia, PA.

Gama-Phola Phonograph. (Value G)

Excello Phonograph in Original Box. (Value G)

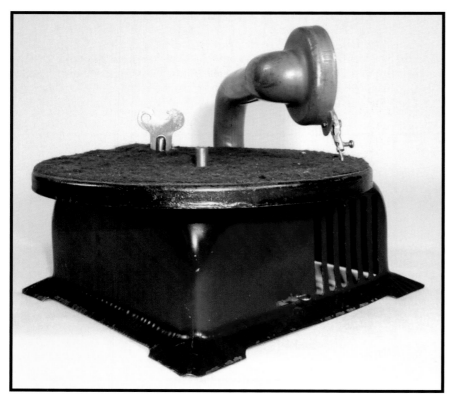

MARVEL JR. TOY PHONOGRAPH

This Marvel Jr. Toy was made in the 1920s by A.B. Cumming Co. in Attleboro, MA. It is key wound and has a very plain tin base, with a green painted tone arm and reproducer. The Baby Jennette phonograph is very similar to the Marvel Toy, with a different style grill and tone arm. These phonographs were made to entice parents and children alike to play 78 rpm records on these small phonographs.

Marvel Jr. Toy. John & Frances Wiedey Collection. (Value F)

MARX PHONOGRAPH

This blue heavy gauge metal phonograph is made by Louis Marx & Co., 200 Fifth Ave., New York. It has an electric motor, automatic brake and a compact tone arm with horizontal reproducer. It also has a built in needle cup for storing needles for the many children's records that would be played on this wonderful blue phonograph.

Marx Phonograph & Tone arm. Bob & Wendie Coon Collection. (Value I)

BING CROSBY JUNIOR JUKE BOX

It was Juke Box Saturday night for parents and children alike. Everybody was dancing to the big band sounds and listening to the crooning of Bing Crosby. The "Bing Crosby Junior Juke" was made in the late 1940s. Curved plastic panels decorated the front of the Juke Box. The front panels would light up to gain the attention of the little folks. The tin sides and top were highly decorated with a colorful vine motif and children dancing to the music of the Juke Box.

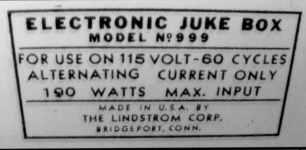

This Electronic Juke Box Model No. 999 was made by the Lindstrom Corp. of Bridgeport, Conn. The bright yellow plastic front panel was the focal point for the on-off control found on the front of this junior Wurlitzer. The playing compartment of this electronic toy had a crystal pickup that played 78 rpm records via a small, tube amplifier. This was not the automatic juke box that you put a nickel in; instead children would place their records on the turntable through the open front compartment. They put on their favorite records and danced the night away until bedtime.

Bing Crosby Juke Box. Robin & Joan Rolfs Collection. (Value E)

BURKAW - KIDDI-TROLA PHONOGRAPH

Little Bo-Peep would enjoy finding her sheep on this child's electric phonograph manufactured by the Burkaw Electric Company of New York in the 1940's. No winding for the little tyke who was lucky to own this modern phonograph to play nursery rhymes on. Typical of many low cost children's phonographs of this period, it employed an A.C. motor driving a turntable with an acoustic reproducer. Another variation of the phonograph is made by Herold Manufacturing Co. It is a larger version and has the identical Little Bo-Peep decal. It was called the Kiddi-trola "Playmate" model child's phonograph.

Burkaw Phonograph. Gfell Family Collection. (Value H)

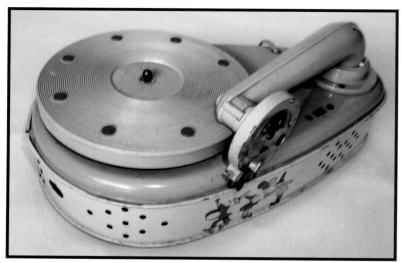

Spear Phonograph. Bob & Wendie Coon Collection. (Value H)

SPEAR PHONOGRAPH

To enchant every child with music, inexpensive electric phonographs were marketed. The same characters are dancing on the Spear phonograph as the Lindstrom phonograph. The Spear model #400 was made in Bridgeport, Conn. A warning was printed on the phonograph telling children not to play warped records.

LINDSTROM PHONOGRAPH

Two colorful electric phonographs from the late 1940s were made by the Lindstrom Corporation of Bridgeport, Conn. Childlike figures and animals decorate these early electric phonographs with acoustic reproducer. The Lindstrom records predate these children's phonographs.

Lindstrom Phonographs. Bob & Wendie Coon Collection. (Value H)

Dupli-Kut Record. (Value H)

DUPLI-KUT & PIX RECORDS

Uncle Joe "The Story Teller" told nursery rhymes in narrative form on the Dupli-Kut Records. The records were advertised as a plastic record that represented a new development in the recording field. The 10 inch records were designed for electrical phonographs. The plastic picture record was laminated to a cardboard backing that gave directions for playing the record on the proper phonograph with the correct needles. It also gave the lyrics and notes of the song that was recorded on the record. A coordinated tape border protected the record. Records were available in album sets. The Pix "Talking Picture" records were identical to the Dupli-Kut Records of 1941.

Pix Record. Lyle Boehland Collection. (Value H)

Merry Go Sound Phonograph. Robin & Joan Rolfs Collection. (Value F)

MERRY GO SOUND PHONOGRAPH

The records go around and around on this Merry Go Sound phonograph toy of 1946. The entire turntable is a merry-go-round and the animals and nursery rhyme characters went for a ride as the record played. It was like going to the amusement park every day of the week. The patents were licensed by Radio Corporation of America and Tone Products Corporation of America.

Identification Label Found on Instrument.

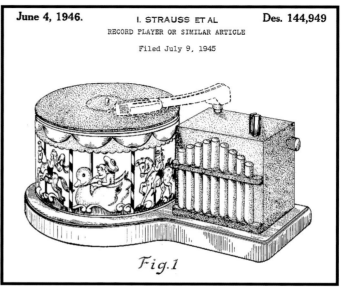

June 4, 1946.   I. STRAUSS ET AL   Des. 144,949

RECORD PLAYER OR SIMILAR ARTICLE

Filed July 9, 1945

Fig.1

Design Patent Drawing 1946 Filed by I. Strauss.

78 RPM Character Record Albums. Bruce Zeeman Collection. (Value I)

BOZO AND FRIENDS

Everybody loves a clown! Bozo was no exception. There were 78 rpm and 45 rpm albums for children of the late 1940s to enjoy. The stories found Bozo "Under the Sea," "On The Farm," "At The Circus" and even in his own "Rocket Ship." The albums were issued in 1949 by Capitol Records. The Capitol Record-Reader took children around the world with story and song. A Bozo talking doll was made in 1964 by Mattel. Bozo talking puppets were made in 1965 by Mattel and 1967 by Sears. Sears also made a Bozo Patter Pal in 1970. Other cartoon characters also came to life in the Capitol Record-Reader. Woody Woodpecker had a talent show as the child would turn the pages at Woody's cue and enjoy the talents of Woody and his friends. Sound effects added to the stories' excitement and children could learn to read and enjoy the stories of their favorite cartoon friends. Bugs Bunny of Looney Tunes fame was entertaining in Storyland Albums. Mel Blanc portrayed the Looney Toons characters of Bugs Bunny, Porky Pig and Daffy Duck as they were up to tricks on records and in the stories.

Bozo 45 RPM Record Album.
Gfell Family Collection. (Value I)

Vogue Record Album V-106 "For The Children". Larry & Sandy Crandell Collection. (Value G)

VOGUE PICTURE RECORDS

The Trial of "Bumble" The Bee, Part I and Part 2, and *The Boy Who Cried Wolf*, Part I and Part 2 are featured on these picturesque ten inch records. Vogue records were made in Michigan by Sav-Way Industries from late 1945-1947. The first issue of these picture records was released on May 6, 1946. These records are the most colorful 78 records recorded for the adult audience. The clear vinyl surface over the sturdy aluminum base plays very well. Although an ideal medium for children's records, only one Vogue album was made for children. The album V-106 "For the Children" was made in 1946. James Jewell, writer and producer of Jack Armstrong, "The All-American Boy" produced it. The orchestra was directed by Hunter Kahler. The records numbers are R-745 and R-746. The bumblebees are pictured on trial with a grasshopper lawyer bringing Bumble, the bee to trial. The well known classic of *The Boy Who Cried Wolf* is depicted with the wolf and the little boy. The little boy runs to the blacksmith who is making horseshoes. Of course, we all know the little boy cried wolf once too often and it is a tale that teaches children to always tell the truth. These records are pieces of artwork set to music.

VALENTINE GREETINGS

Valentine Cards (Value I each)

As a matter of RECORD I want you to be my Valentine. February 14th is a day when school children would exchange Valentines and phonographs put their Valentine greetings on record.

Promotional Photo. Lowell Gearhart Collection. (Value H)

Sonora Adv. Doll. (Value I)

Sonora Adv. Doll. (Value I)

COLLECTIVE IMAGINATION

The joy of childhood imagination is captured by this photo of children gleefully listening to records being played on the home phonograph. The young lad in charge of selecting the program has obviously made a big hit with the youngsters. One can only imagine what thoughts are stimulated in the minds of the children as Christmas Eve approaches.

Most major record companies found it profitable to produce music and stories for the juvenile audience. Perhaps the Victor Company found that a photograph such as this could help promote sales of post war radio-phonograph combination products when strategically placed in dealer locations. The Sonora Phonograph Company had the Sonora Twins and Sonora Doll to promote their latest hits on Sonora records.

CHAPTER 3

BABY BOOMER TOYS FROM THE
1950s - 1960s

The "Baby Boomers" have arrived. It is the Rock & Roll fabulous 50s. The post-war economy is booming and the market for toys is hot. Only one doll company name survives from the 1940s. It is the EFFanBEE Company. The EFFanBEE Company is soon joined by new names like Mattel, Hasbro and Ideal Toy Corporation. The familiar crank of the 1940s gave way to key wind, pull string or the push of a button. Compact battery operated electric motors and emerging electronics replaced many of the manual wind up mechanisms. Records are made of plastic and are "unbreakable." The dolls are also unbreakable, but the pull strings and push buttons are often found in broken condition today. Many of the dolls of this age were mass-produced and this was the beginning of the disposable era and planned obsolescence marketing. This chapter represents the more significant phonograph dolls from the 1950s and 1960s. Many talking dolls were made and excellent reference books have been written documenting each and every doll of the 1950s and 1960s.

SCHILLING DOLL

The doll with the baby face and pink dress was an immensely popular doll of the 1950s. The Joseph L. Schilling Toy Company made this doll. She was a phenomenal success when she was introduced for the 1949 Christmas season. According to a report in the 1949 *Playthings*, this was the result of a test market for the doll. "The promotion started on the morning of July 7th. At 11 AM the next day, the store reordered 600 more dolls. On July 18th, it reordered 1,200 more. On August 21st, it asked that 600 more be flown in immediately. On August 25, the same store pushed through a demand for 10,000 dolls for delivery before Christmas. Thus, in a city of only 150,000 people (Peoria, Ill.) one store had sold more than 12,500 of the Shilling dolls in its first season. Nationwide promotions effected a similar response and several million talking dolls were sold by Christmas." To meet the demand, Schilling added three New York factories and three California factories to a single factory in each state where the dolls were originally manufactured.

The Schilling doll is 21 inches tall. She has molded painted hair. Some Schilling dolls were available with a mohair or synthetic wig. Her head is made of hard plastic, while the arms and legs are soft vinyl. The doll body is cloth. Her baby face has sleep eyes with real lashes above and painted ones below. She has two teeth and a big smile. Her dress could be found in a choice of pink or blue trimmed with Ninon lace with a matching bonnet. A.F. Ciffo designed the doll. A purple ribbon sash with the company's name completed her dress.

Schilling Doll. Bessie & Floyd Seiter Collection. (Value F)

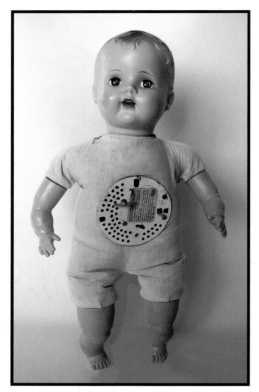

Schilling Doll Showing Motor in Front.

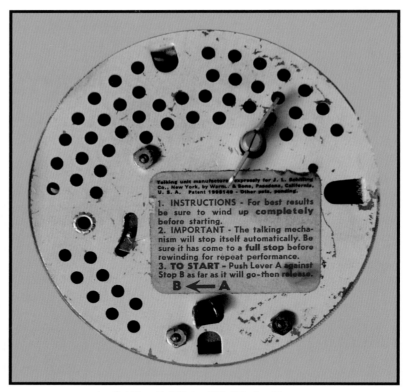

Schilling Doll Motor With Winding Key.

To operate the doll, the child must first wind the phonograph by means of a key. Many times the doll would start to talk while winding. This meant that the doll was not wound completely on previous use and did not shut off. By gently squeezing a small lever the reproducer is returned to the beginning of the record and the Schilling doll will talk, laugh, cry and sob. The children were told to ignore the motor noise, as it will diminish as the talking unit is broken in. The motor operates the small turntable by means of a rubber band that becomes brittle and breaks with age. This can be replaced and the doll will talk once again. Excellent directions and a guarantee were provided to children with each doll. A small plastic record plays back the voice of the Schilling doll. The talking unit was designed by J. J. Warner. A key wound spring powers the phonograph mechanism. The stamped metal phonograph is identified: TALKING UNIT/ WARNER & CO. 300 N. LAKE, PASADENA PAT. 1998149 - OTHER PAT. PENDING.

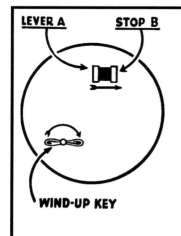

HOW TO MAKE DOLL TALK

1—Wind up with key on back of doll. Be sure to *fully* wind up when starting for *best* results.

2—To start—Push lever A against Stop B as far as it will go. (See diagram.)

3—*IMPORTANT*—The talking mechanism will stop itself automatically. Be sure it has come to a full stop before rewinding for repeat performance.

Made in the USA by American Labor and of American Material.

Directions on "How to Make Doll Talk".

Schilling Doll Motor and Record.

Variations of the Schilling doll can be found. Many times these dolls are not marked. They vary in size and gender. The phonograph mechanism can be found mounted in the front or back of the doll. Both have the same Warner motor within their cloth body.

In addition to bringing smiles to children, the Schilling doll helped aid the veterans of World War II. She was the prize in a raffle to aid veterans and care for war orphans. This Schilling doll was the beginning of dolls for the "Baby Boomer" generation of the 1950s. The Schilling doll was advertised as the talking doll with the genuine human voice. "So real it startles you."

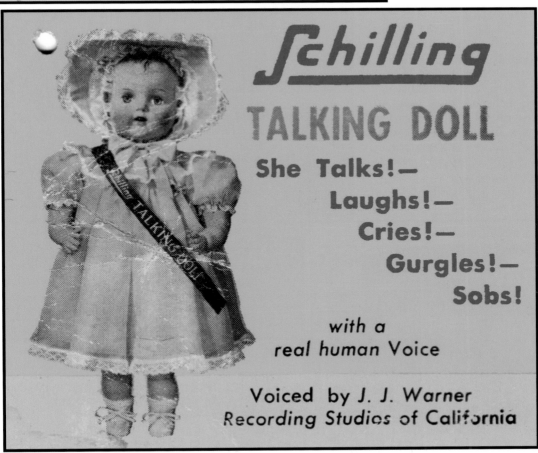

Guarantee Tag Attached to Each Schilling Doll. Bessie and Floyd Seiter Collection. (Value I)

NOMA DOLL

The EFFanBEE Company was sold to Noma Electric in 1946. Noma was well known for its Christmas tree lights. In December of 1950 the Noma doll was placed on the market. She continued to be manufactured for three years and was later known as "Noma, The Electronic Doll." This Noma doll originally had a wrist tag with the name "Playmate." Her hard plastic swivel head is marked EFFanBEE. This doll has a cloth body with soft vinyl plastic arms and legs that discolor with age. She has bright red lips with an open mouth showing two front teeth and a felt tongue. Noma may be found with molded hair or a synthetic wig. She is a tall 28 inch baby doll. She is dressed in a 1950s style pink dress with puff sleeves. It is accented with checked fabric collar, vest and band on her skirt. The fabric is silk-like acetate. A matching bonnet trimmed with pink ribbon completes her outfit. Noma plays a 3 1/2 inch plastic 78 rpm record with a steel needle fastened to a paper diaphragm. The turntable is belt driven by a small Noma Electric three-volt motor. The die cast motor housing does not age well and is often found to be warped or broken. The mechanism is housed in a removable pink plastic compartment found in the chest of the doll. The motor is marked "Noma Electric Corporation, New York, N.Y."

Noma Doll, Original Dress.
Robin & Joan Rolfs Collection. (Value F)

Noma Doll Motor. Larry Hudson Collection. (Value H)

At a push of a button Noma speaks very distinctly. To some she was known as the talking creature. Her start button is very sensitive; the slightest press can set Noma talking. She can repeat her forty-seven second speech hundreds of times or as long as the batteries last. She will recite the following to the delight of her owner:

"My name is Noma, and Mommy taught me to recite. Mary had a little lamb, her fleece was white as snow, and everywhere that Mary went, the lamb was sure to go. I can sing, too. London Bridge is falling down, falling down, falling down. London Bridge is falling down, my fair lady. (Laughs) I can't sing the rest mommy, cause I'm tired, so I'll say my prayers and go to bed. Now I lay me down to sleep. I pray the Lord my soul to keep, and if I should not live, I pray the Lord my soul to take. Goodnight mommy and daddy and everybody."

Noma Doll Advertisement. Circa 1950. (Value I)

The "Noma Talking, Walking Doll" was advertised as being "electronic with a real human voice." In fact, the doll is not electronic, nor does she walk. The sound reproduction is mechanical but the motor operating the turntable is battery powered. The tiny motor armature is made of laminated silicone steel to increase its efficiency. Noma is an automatic starter. The child only has to press a button and the turntable starts setting the needle to the beginning of the record. It was reported that the popular ventriloquist, Edgar Bergen, on introducing Noma at an auction for the benefit of blind children, pressed the button, listened for a moment and turning to his audience remarked, "What am I doing? This sort of thing may put me out of business." A full one page advertisement promotes the EFFanBEE Noma doll. The ad exclaims Noma is an "electronic" doll with a real human voice. She was a sensational doll in the 1950s.

WAL-FELD PHONOGRAPH

This 1950s phonograph enthralled children with its blue base with the Cat and the Fiddle, the Tin Man and the Scarecrow from the Wizard of Oz and Mother Goose. The red turntable with the light colored acoustical reproducer played the songs illustrated on this colorful child's phonograph.

Wal-Feld Phonograph. Gfell Family Collection. (Value H)

BO-PEEP DOLL

Little Bo-Peep is a small 10 1/2 inch talking storybook doll. She is plastic with painted eyes and lashes. Bo-Peep is known for her blond ringlets of rooted hair. Her mouth is open showing her four front teeth. She wears a blue dress with a gingham puff apron. She also has a matching gingham bonnet. White shoes and tights complete her outfit. She is a pull cord talker and speaks up to eleven phrases as she is looking for her sheep. Little Bo-Peep and Cinderella are part of this Storybook doll series by Mattel Toys of 1969.

Bo-Peep Doll. (Value H)

PORTABLE PHONOGRAPH

Phonographs made for the children's market were made by various manufacturers. Many were not marked and were sold as promotions by department stores. This highly decorated portable phonograph is not marked with a manufacturer's label. The graphics found inside and out captured children's imagination as they played their records on this portable phonograph. A generic reproducer is found on this nifty portable. The child needed to change needles after every three plays and crank the motor properly to hear the sounds of the record.

Portable Phonograph. Gfell Family Collection. (Value H)

Davy Crockett Phonograph (Value G) & Records (Value I). Bob & Wendie Coon Collection.

Plastic Battery Operated Phonograph. Maker Unknown.
John & Frances Wiedey Collection. (Value I)

DAVY CROCKETT PHONOGRAPH

The Ballad of Davy Crockett, "King of the Wild Frontier," rang out from the Davy Crockett phonograph. The yellow plastic compact phonograph was proudly marked with Davy Crockett and his musket on the front of the phonograph. Young explorers let their imagination take them to the wild frontier with their hero, Davy Crockett. A variety of Davy Crockett records were marketed by Little Golden Records and the Columbia Record Company. There was even a picture record of Davy Crockett by Record Guild of America. If a child could not afford the Davy Crockett phonograph, many other inexpensive plastic phonographs were available.

MECHANICAL TOY PHONOGRAPH

Plastic phonographs of red and blue coloration are found in their original boxes. This compact keywind phonograph is made in the U.S.A. by Louis Marx and Co. of New York. The entire phonograph is plastic including the tone arm and reproducer. The key and turntable are metal. These inexpensive plastic toys brought hours of enjoyment to children as they played their colorful new records also made of the new material -- plastic.

Marx Mechanical Toy Phonograph in Original Box. Bob & Wendie Coon Collection. (Value H)

Twirl-a-Tune Phonograph. John & Frances Wiedey Collection. (Value G)

TWIRL-A-TUNE

Fun galore was in store for the child who received this bright red phonograph in the red box. The child would need to demonstrate a coordinated effort to twirl the turntable at a regular speed to hear the records. The base is made of wood. A cardboard horn with a scalloped edge and graphics of notes, flowers and pets is attached to the reproducer. It was made by Colorgraphic of Chicago, Ill. The child who owned this T w i r l - A - T u n e phonograph kept it in pristine condition in the original box.

WINNIE DOLL

The Winnie doll is a technological marvel. Her banner hails her as, "Winnie THE UNAIDED WALKING & TALKING DOLL." It was in 1953 when the Advance Doll and Toy Co. added voice technology to their line of walking dolls. Winnie had an older sister, Wanda, that walked by herself, but did not talk. Wanda was the 1951 introduction of the unaided walking doll.

Winnie Doll Guarantee Certificate, Direction Packet & Records. (Value H)

Winnie was made by the Advance Doll & Toy Company. There has been little history found on this company. One day we received an inquiry from Bill Chambers regarding the availability of a Tama doll. He wanted a Tama Doll for his wife "Tama." He stated that the doll was originally named for his wife. We instantly wrote Bill and inquired if his wife was indeed the real Tama. She is the real Tama and here is a brief history of the company:

This is the story of Mr. Edward Ardolino, his daughter Tama and the Advance Doll and Toy Company. Edward Ardolino is of Italian descent and grew up in West Haven, Connecticut. He is one of eight children. Like most young men of his generation, he served in the armed forces during World War II. In approximately 1945, Ed's father started a small business called Universal Metal Stamping at 106 Water St. in West Haven, Connecticut. The company produced small parts by stamping metal with heavy presses and custom-made dies. When Ed returned from his military service, he joined his father, brothers and sisters at the company. In 1947 the company became Universal Industries and included the original metal stamping business as well as a new company named, The Advance Doll & Toy Company.

Winnie Doll With Original Box.
Robin & Joan Rolfs Collection. (Value F)

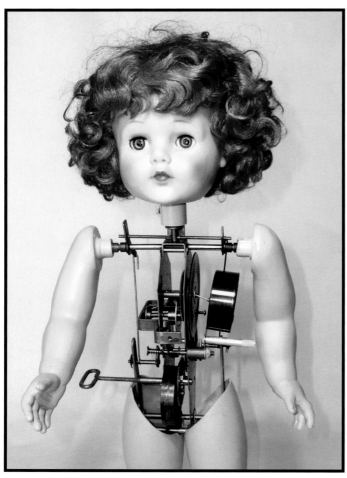

Winnie Doll With Body Panels Removed Exposing
the Complex Clockwork Mechanism.

The toy company produced small metal toys using the stamping process of the parent company. In 1951 Advance Doll and Toy Company introduced Wanda, a wind up doll capable of walking unaided. In 1953 they added voice technology to their product line and introduced Winnie. In order to give the dolls a natural voice they needed to solve the problem of controlling the speed of the wind up spring motor. The spring drove the voice mechanism very fast when it was tight and then the voice slowed as the spring unwound. To solve this problem of speed variation, the Ardolino's designed a small constant-speed governor that gave a smooth natural speed to her voice as well as her walk. A knurled knob protruding from her left side engages the key wind mechanism.

She is 26 inches in height and quite heavy for children to handle. She has a hard plastic two-piece body and vinyl or hard plastic head. The walking and talking mechanism is found within her body shell. Winnie was available as a blond or brunette. Her sleep eyes have real upper lashes and painted lower lashes. She says, "Hi, my name is Winnie; I can walk, I can talk; Mommy please pick me up; I'm so tired; I can sing too." She sings "The Farmer in the Dell" and "Jack & Jill." Her records can be interchanged to say different phrases. Replacement records were available from the company. A single replacement was 35 cents. A three record album of assorted rhymes and jingles was $1.00.

Winnie Doll Mechanism, Showing Record
and Speaker Diaphragm.

Almost every little girl of the 1950s dreamed of wearing a bridal dress on her wedding day. To help them envision this special day, the Winnie doll came adorned in a gorgeous white satin bride dress with a V-shape neckline. Pink flowers accented the neckline. A stunning veil and headpiece completed this beautiful bridal outfit worn by Winnie on her wedding day.

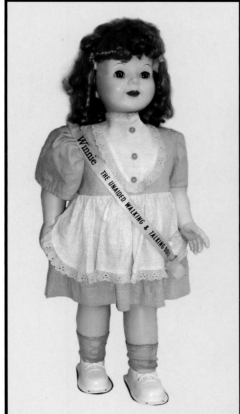

Early Winnie Doll.
Warren E. Kelm Collection.
(Value F)

An early version of Winnie is dressed in a cotton dress with a white inset accented with ruffles and three aqua buttons. A white apron added a fashion touch to her skirted dress. Later models of Winnie are dressed in a satin blue or pink dress with ruffles at the bottom of the skirt. A velvet ribbon accents her waistline and collar. Her shoes are non-removable incorporating an ingenious roller and ratchet device for walking.

Winnie Bride Doll. Deanna Danner Collection. (Value F)

Tama Dolls in White Poodle Dress & Red Sailboat Dress. Robin & Joan Rolfs Collection. (Value F)

TAMA DOLL

The Tama doll was introduced in 1954 and was named for Tama Ardolino. Her creator was Tama's father, Edward Ardolino of the Advance Doll and Toy Company, West Haven, Connecticut. She was smaller than Winnie, only 23 inches tall. Tama has a soft vinyl head, arms and legs. Her body is cloth. She has blue sleep eyes with real upper lashes and painted lower lashes. Her synthetic hair is nicely curled. A banner is pinned across the front of her dress that reads: "TAMA THE TALKING DOLL."

Tama Doll Motor. Bessie & Floyd Seiter Collection.

Tama uses the same voice mechanism as Winnie. The doll was designed to be a soft cuddly friend for a little girl, something she could easily carry and care for. The phonograph is located in the front of her body. It is a key wind mechanism encased in a rigid cardboard box with slotted openings for the speaker. A knurled knob is turned to bring the reproducer to the beginning of the record and start the motor. The spring wound talking mechanism plays small three inch records that are interchangeable. This gives Tama the capability to do a variety of activities such as teaching nursery rhymes, singing songs, and praying. Tama's voice was recorded by the singer Edie Adams, wife of Ernie Kovacs. Recordings were made at Columbia Records Studio in New York and were produced by the Columbia facility in Bridgeport, Connecticut.

Tama Doll Record and Speaker.

Tama Doll Motor and Reproducer.

MELODIE DOLL

Melodie is an EFFanBEE doll made from 1953 to 1956. Pull down a cover plate on the doll's back and the child had access to the battery operated phonograph that made Melodie talk. Her phonograph played black disc records. Her knees had special joints, that enabled her to kneel while she recited, "Now I Lay Me Down to Sleep." This feature earned her the name of the prayer doll.

Records titles that the Melodie doll plays are:

Lullaby Prayer
One, Two, Buckle My Shoe
Simple Simon
Eensie Weensie Spider
Four and Twenty Blackbirds
Sing a Song of Six Pence
Twinkle, Twinkle, Little Star
Rock A Bye Baby

Melodie Doll. Robin & Joan Rolfs Collection. (Value G)

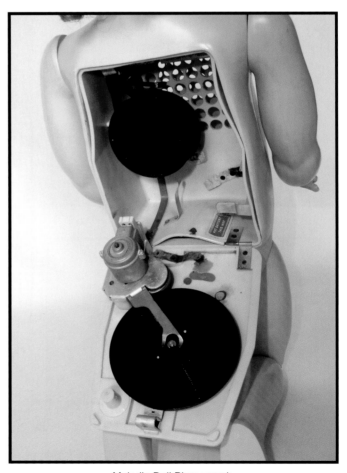

Melodie Doll Phonograph.

Melodie is a big girl measuring 27 inches high. Her vinyl head has blond synthetic rooted hair. Her arms, legs, and body are hard plastic. She has piercing blue eyes with real lashes. Her dress styles vary. She may be seen wearing a straw hat coordinating with her pink nylon dress trimmed with pink ribbon. She also can be found in a formal dusty blue dress trimmed with pink flowers and ribbons. This EFFanBEE doll came with a heart shaped tag stating; "I am MELODIE, The Talking Doll With The Golden Voice. An EFFanBEE Adorable Doll." The child had a challenging task of changing records and batteries to make Melodie sing and talk.

Name That Tune Game. Pat Zeeman Collection. (Value I)

NAME THAT TUNE GAME

"Name That Tune," host George De Witt would exclaim on the CBS TV show of the 1950s. Milton Bradley marketed a music bingo game with over 160 excerpts from the world's finest melodies on a 33 1/3 rpm hi-fi record pressed and recorded by Columbia transcriptions. This 1957 game was for children ages 10 to adult. Listen to a few bars of a popular song and see if you can...Name That Tune!

Zany Phonograph. (Value I)

ZANY HAND WIND PHONOGRAPH

This Zany hand wind portable phonograph was ready to play. The celluloid horn and reproducer are all in one. It was a new plastic toy for children! It was advertised to play five, seven and ten inch records. It came in a cardboard box that doubled as a carrying case, complete with a cardboard handle. This toy was made in St. Louis, MO. It was an AZ LINE TOY of the 1950s.

Magic Mirror Movies Toy With Red Raven Records. Robin & Joan Rolfs Collection. (Value G)

MAGIC MIRROR MOVIES TOY

The Magic Mirror Movies toy consisted of records and a Magic Mirror carousel made up of fifteen 1/2 X 1 1/4 inch mirrors. The mirror segments are made of a high quality plastic. On the bottom of the Magic Mirror carousel is a hole that enables the Magic Mirror to be placed over the turntable spindle. Before placing the Magic Mirror on the turntable the child would select a Magic Mirror record. The animated illustrations are ingeniously synchronized to the music and reflect from the record onto the revolving Magic Mirror. This was a simple toy to use. The child would just place the record on the turntable in the usual way; slip the Magic Mirror on top of the spindle and play! The Magic Mirror toy plays on any single-play 78 rpm record player. It was a product of Morgan Development Laboratories Inc. of Westport, Connecticut. The company advertised this $3.00 Magic Mirror Movies toy as used by, "leading Child Scientists for visual and rhythmic training --- the 3-dimensional pictures develop the senses of perspective, color and motion --- the action synchronized to music develops a sense of rhythm!" There are three packaging styles for this Magic Mirror Movies toy.

Bottom of Red Raven Magic Mirror Carousel

Early Version of Magic Mirror Movies Toy. (Value G)

Red Raven Magic Mirror Movies Toy. Patd. Canada-1961. (Value G)

The Red Raven trademark is found on each record. This Red Raven trademark is also found on the bottom of the Magic Mirror toy. The praxinoscopic device was patented by Porter S. Morgan in 1956. The records were made from 1956 through the early 1960s. They were manufactured by Vox Imago, Morgan Development Laboratories of Connecticut. The first records produced were made of flexible cardboard with a brass grommet around the center hole and a rolled metal edge. Later records were made of colored vinyl with pictures around the center. Others were made of clear vinyl with a large illustrated paper label. Records were made for every occasion: Christmas, Halloween, birthday parties and fun records of frogs leaping, ducks swimming or Little Bo-Peep finding her sheep. The records were processed by Bing Crosby Phonocards Inc., N.Y.C. and were distributed by Childhood Interests, Inc., Roselle Park, New Jersey. They could only be played on a 78 rpm record player with a standard electric (not acoustic) tone arm and sold for approximately 75 cents.

RED RAVEN JUKE BOX

A novelty tin toy Juke Box Bank made by HAJI of Japan plays a Red Raven Movie record. Insert a penny and the record spins around and 'round making a tinkling sound as the Red Raven saves your pennies to buy the real Red Raven Movie records.

Juke Box With Red Raven Movie Record in Original Box. (Value G)

The tin Red Raven movie record on the jukebox bank spins when a penny is inserted. This record has the same Red Raven logo as the children's records made for the Magic Mirror Movies toy. The record is permanently attached to the 3 3/4 X 4 1/2 inch "Select-O-Matic" jukebox.

ACTION VIEWER

The Action Viewer is an imitation of the Magic Mirror Movies Toy. The eight-sided Viewer mirror was simple in design. On the top of the mirror, instructions told the child to "PLACE RECORD ON TURNTABLE -- PLACE ACTION VIEWER ON RECORD." This toy was manufactured by Record Pressing and Recording Corp., N.Y. 18, N.Y. The Action Viewer came with the unbreakable plastic viewer plus a free record. The records were made by the Record Guild of America. Records were available as single records or they could be purchased as sets in a carrying case, a record chest with rack, a deluxe album or a deluxe chest. The animated picture discs are six inches in diameter.

Action Viewer Toy. Robin & Joan Rolfs Collection. (Value F)

3-18

Jambo the Jiver in Original Box.
Bessie & Floyd Seiter Collection. (Value G)

Talentoon Record for Jambo the Jiver.
Bessie & Floyd Seiter Collection.

JAMBO THE JIVER

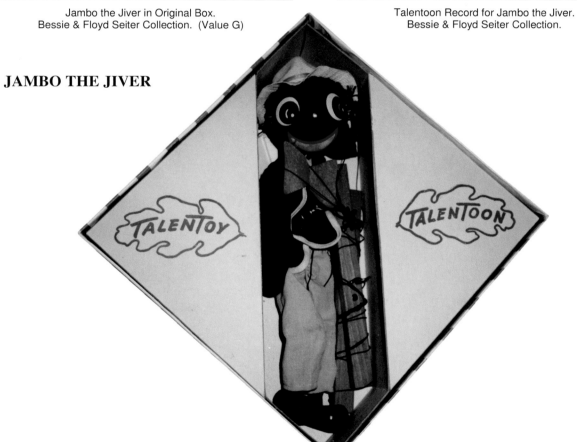

Jambo the Jiver is one of four marionettes made by EFFanBEE Doll Co. in 1952. The others are Kilroy, Toonga, and Pimbo. Jambo is attached to wood crosspieces by many strings and can be made to walk or dance by the use of one hand as he jives to the tune of a 78 rpm record being played on a phonograph. The record is a Talentoon made by Talent Product, Inc., New York. Side one is *Jambo The Jiver* by Paul Hammond and side two is *Jambo Jive* by Michael Chimes Harmonix. The directions explain that the figure is a marionette that really comes to life as he dances to the music.

General Electric Play-Talk Electronic Recording Toy. John & Frances Wiedey Collection. (Value G)

Gem Recordmaker. Gfell Family Collection. (Value H)

RECORD MAKERS

Little tykes loved their toy phonographs, but they also wanted to make their own recordings and record the voices of their friends. The General Electric Play-Talk Toy has a magnetic recorder incorporated into the record/playback head mounted on the end of the tone arm. This recording head records on thin paper discs coated with an iron oxide material. The recording kit contains the yellow and blue phonograph/recorder with a decal showing children making their own records. A separate speaker and extra recording discs were part of this total General Electric Play-Talk toy.

The Recordmaker of 1958 by the Gem Color Inc. Company of Paterson, New Jersey taunted that "you could make your own permanent records in a jiffy." The Recordmaker came with a complete recording machine, recording head and Gem Recordmaker recording records. The instructions for set-up stated that a child could set up this Recordmaker in a jiffy and have the fun of recording their own songs, nursery rhymes and voices of their friends.

Miniature Teen Figures Listening
to Phonograph. (Value I)

Record Tote Bag.
Bob & Wendie Coon Collection. (Value I)

Record totes, miniature figures, games and musical cards were a few of the novelties that teens of the 1950s could purchase to decorate their room, carry their records to a friend's house or send a music box birthday card from Barker Music Box Cards of Cincinnati, Ohio to that special someone.

Musical Phonograph Card. Becky Zeeman Collection. (Value I)

Carnival Phonograph Toy. John & Frances Wiedey Collection. (Value H)

CARNIVAL TOY

This compact child's record player was fun and educational for children. Records for the Carnival toy phonograph came in sets of four. The player has an adjustable playing speed. It runs on a single "D" cell flashlight battery. The child could listen to 600 plays per battery. No winding needed. Just take this compact phonograph with you wherever you go. It could entertain a child in the car, on the beach or at grandmother's house. The records are small and are inserted into the side of the red compact phonograph. It has an automatic shut off. This small phonograph was made by Carnival Toy Mfg. Corp., Division of Lorraine Industries Inc. of Bridgeport, Conn.

LITTLE JOHN RECORDS

The 1950s initiated the age of plastics. The Little John records were made in intense hues of colored vinyl. These five inch records were made by Precision Plastics Co. of Philadelphia, PA. Catchy songs such as: *Z-I-P Went The Rocket Ship; Little Polly Polite; Doll's Tea Party; Billy Boy; Farmer in the Dell; Funny Circus Clown; Paper Doll; Couldn't Cry; Jimminy Crickety Boo;* and *Here Come the Cowboys*, are representative of some of the songs recorded for children. For special occasions there were: *Happy Birthday; Merry Christmas Song; I Heard the Bells on Christmas Day;* and *Joy to the World*. For pennies children could enjoy their songs on these bright unbreakable 78 rpm records.

Little John Records. (Value I)

CHATTY CATHY

The Mattel Toy Company is the most prolific manufacturer of talking dolls. Starting with the first issue of Chatty Cathy in 1959, versions of this popular doll continue to be reissued into the twenty-first century. This was the doll of the baby boomers. There are complete reference books dedicated to Chatty Cathy dolls and the Mattel Toy Company. We will only touch on some of the Mattel dolls employing talking mechanisms. These dolls are important to the history of phonograph dolls and highly prized by doll collectors.

Chatty Cathy Dolls in Pin Stripe and Pink Dress.
John & Frances Wiedey Collection. (Value F)

Chatty Cathy was made to represent a four or five year old child. She is 19 inches tall with a vinyl or hard plastic head, body and limbs. The first Chatty Cathy is known to have darker skin than the later Chatty Cathy. She has sleep eyes and freckles on her nose. Her mouth is slightly open revealing two buckteeth. Both blond and brunette dolls were made with either blue or brown eyes. She is the typical little girl with the popular pageboy hairstyle, freckles, protruding tummy, knobby knees and in a word: "Cute." Chatty had many outfits and loved to have her dresses changed. The clothes were all adorable on Chatty Cathy and made especially for her.

The value of Chatty Cathy dolls is based on the working condition of the voice mechanism, condition of the doll and original dress. Unfortunately many of the dolls are found with the talking mechanism broken. The pull string was not the most durable part of this talking doll. The mechanism can be replaced; however it is not easy to get to the working parts of the doll as they are encased in a two-piece hard plastic shell with welded seams.

Chatty Cathy in Party Dress.
Bessie & Floyd Seiter Collection. (Value F)

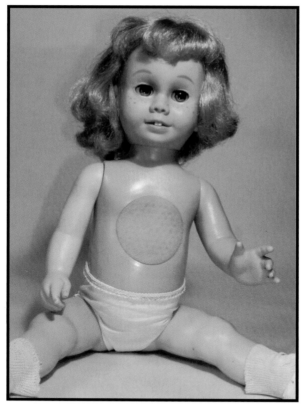

Chatty Cathy With Cloth Speaker in Chest.
Bessie & Floyd Seiter Collection

There are five issues of Chatty Cathy. The first issue was made in 1959 and marketed in 1960. This doll has the grill covered with a tan cloth. She was unmarked and perhaps sold as a prototype. The second issue is the same as the first, except it is marked with a rectangle on its back, which states "CHATTY CATHY PATENTS PENDING MCMLX BY MATTEL, INC. HAWTHORNE, CALIF." The third issue has no covering over the grill, but there is an indented circle around the hexagon speaker. The fourth issue omitted the circle and just has the hexagon speaker. In the fifth issue there are four additional holes added beneath the grill. The first Chatty's spoke eleven sentences, but later her vocabulary was increased to eighteen sentences.

The Chatty talking mechanism is a three inch by five inch box containing a 2 1/2 inch record sealed within her body. There is a coil spring within a spool with a string wrapped around it. When the magic string is pulled, it winds the coil spring much like winding a phonograph. This provides the power for the phonograph motor, which is engaged when the string is released. The tiny needle plays the record and Chatty Cathy speaks. There are two voices for early Chatty Cathy. One is June Foray, which is most common, and the other is Lucille Bliss. The voice of Maureen McCormick was used in the 1969-70 reissue of Chatty Cathy. Chatty's original dress is either a red and white pinafore or a blue party dress. She came with a shoehorn, an eight page booklet and warranty tag.

Little girls love to play "dress up." The Mattel Company made stylish clothing for the Chatty Cathy dolls. They could be dressed up for a party, the playground or bedtime. The Chatty Cathy line of clothing has the "Chatty Cathy T.M. by Mattel," label. She has winter, summer and spring fashion style clothing. Shoes and other accessories were also made available to add the finishing touch to her wardrobe.

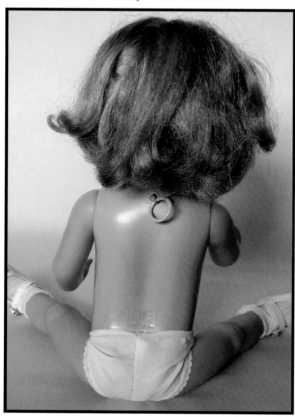

Chatty Cathy Showing the Pull String.

Chatty Cathy Clothing Label.

CHARMIN' CHATTY

Charmin' Chatty is a scholarly looking doll. She made her debut on the market in 1961. Marked TM@1961 Mattel Inc/Hawthorn Calif., USA, Charmin' Chatty came as a blond or a redhead and wore glasses. She is 25 inches tall with long legs and a fairly slim body. Her best known outfit is her sailor suit, red knee socks and white and blue saddle shoes. Charmin' also has other outfits like a "Let's Go Shopping" wardrobe. Charmin' Chatty has changeable records. Five plastic records came with the doll and they can be played by placing them into a slot on her left side. These records gave her a vocabulary of one hundred twenty different phrases. The child inserted a record into the side slot and then pulled a string and Charmin' Chatty started talking. Her five original records are: *Get Acquainted side 1 and 2; Mother/Ridiculous; Scary/Animal Noises; Famous/Good,* and *Poems/Proverbs.* Charmin' Chatty has the famous voice of Maureen McCormick who was Marsha of the Brady Bunch.

Side View of Charmin' Chatty Showing Record Insertion Slot.

Charmin' Chatty Records

Charmin' Chatty. John & Frances Wiedey Collection. (Value G)

MATTY MATTEL AND SISTER BELLE

Matty is 17 inches tall. He has a hard plastic head that houses his voice box. Sister Belle and Matty are twin sister and brother. She is just as tall as Matty. They both have pull string talking mechanisms. They are casually dressed. Matty has his tee shirt and jeans with red cuffs. Sister Belle wears a striped dress with red pockets. They both have cloth shoes that don't get lost. Matty and Sister Belle were 1961 TV cartoon favorites and both speak eleven popular cartoon phrases.

Matty Mattel. (Value G)   Sister Belle. (Value H)
John & Frances Wiedey Collection.

Chatty Baby 1962 (Value H), Tiny Chatty Twins 1963 (Value G), Singin' Chatty 1965 (Value G). John & Frances Wiedey Collection.

CHATTY'S FRIENDS

In 1962 Chatty Baby was added to the Mattel family. Chatty baby is 18 inches tall and wears a red outfit with matching red shoes. Tiny Chatty Baby and Tiny Chatty Brother are 15 inch twins that were added to Chatty Cathy's family in 1963. The Chatty Baby twins wear blue outfits with "Tiny Chatty Baby" embroidered on the girl's bib and boy's shirt. The last of the Chatty Cathy series to be produced was Singin' Chatty. She was made for only one year. The year was 1965 and then the manufacture of all Chatty Cathy dolls ceased. Singin' Chatty is 17 inches tall and wears a red dress. She sings eleven different nursery rhymes such as: *Old MacDonald Had a Farm* and *London Bridge is Falling Down*. She could be purchased with either blond or brunette hair. During the time of their manufacture three black dolls were made: Chatty Cathy, Chatty Baby and Tiny Chatty Baby.   Perhaps Chatty and her friends would sing or talk on their Mattel-O-Phone, which was also made in 1965. This telephone made by Mattel came with many two-sided records.

Tiny Chatty Baby With Box. (Value H)

TICKLES

Spank her and she cries, tickle her and she laughs. This doll made by Deluxe Reading Company was born in 1963. She is a 21 inch hard plastic and vinyl doll. A knob on her right side activates the battery operated mechanism. These dolls are wearing their original dresses with the duck motif. Both dolls have an easy care short haircut that enhances their baby face.

Deluxe Reading Doll.
(Value H)

Tickles Doll in Original Box.   John & Frances Wiedey Collection. (Value G)

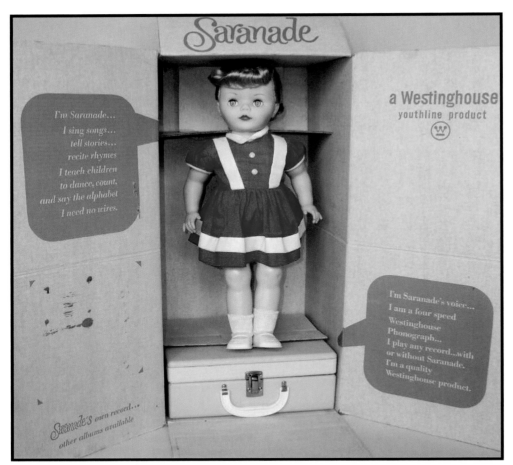

SARANADE DOLL

"I'm Saranade...I sing songs... tell stories, recite rhymes. I teach children to dance, count and say the alphabet. I need no wires." The back of her head is marked: "Uneeda Doll Co. Inc. 1962." She stands 22 inches tall. Saranade was available as either a blond or brunette and has soft rooted hair in her original ponytail style. She has hard plastic legs and body, hard vinyl arms and a soft vinyl head. She has adorable big eyes of blue or brown with beautiful upper eyelashes. Saranade wears a bright red dress with white trim and two buttons down the front. White shoes and socks coordinate with her outfit.

Saranade Doll in Original Box with Westinghouse Phonograph.
Robin & Joan Rolfs Collection. (Value F)

She is definitely a one-of-a-kind phonograph doll with her own portable phonograph. The Westinghouse phonograph is made especially for the Saranade Doll. The Westinghouse phonograph is a four speed record player and will play any record, with or without the Saranade doll. There is a knob on the phonograph, which lets you switch the sound from the phonograph to the doll. It works with a low power A.M. radio transmitter built into the phonograph. There are no wires to make her sing. There is a switch on the doll's tummy that must also be turned on to make Saranade receive the signal from the phonograph. Saranade can stand or sit when she talks. She sounds best when standing within a foot or two of the phonograph. The operation of the doll and phonograph combination may be frustrating for some youngsters as movement of the doll causes the signal to fade out or distort. The concept may be good in technical theory, but in practice may not offer all that it promises.

Saranade 33 RPM Record in Original Sleeve. (Value I)

A Golden Hi-Fi 33 1/3 rpm record is recorded especially for the Saranade Doll. On the record is recorded: *We sing my theme song; We get ready each morning; We read a story; We play a party game; We learn French;* and *We go to bed.* The record sleeve has Saranade on the cover in her red dress. It has the Golden record label and the Westinghouse seal.

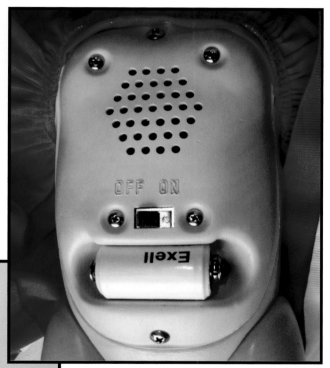

There is an opening in her tummy that holds a 9 volt battery. The switch on her tummy is to turn the doll receiver on and off. There is also a speaker in her chest, which conveys the songs and stories that Saranade tells.

Saranade can sit on your lap and as you look into her cute face she sings and talks to you. No wires, just the songs and rhymes coming from the Saranade doll. It must have been an amazing sensation for the 1960s. Saranade is the perfect name for this doll that can win your heart with her bright eyes, smile and a song.

Little Miss Echo. John & Frances Wiedey Collection. (Value F)

LITTLE MISS ECHO

This doll echoes whatever you say to her. Little Miss Echo is a tall 30 inches and was made by the American Character Doll Company in 1965. Little Miss Echo uses two D-size flashlight batteries and one standard nine volt transistor battery. To record, you turn the decorative red knob at the doll's neck counterclockwise and wait for a "Beep." Talk until the "Beep" sounds again and turn the knob to the center immediately. Your words are recorded on a magnetic tape loop. To play back, turn the knob clockwise and the message will continue to play back until the decorative red knob is turned to the center position. Little Miss Echo repeats your words and songs in your own voice. She is truly Little Miss Echo.

DROWSY

Drowsy is a 1965 popular doll that children loved at bedtime. At first she was dressed in pajamas with a kitten motif, but in 1968 her outfit was changed to pink pajamas with white polka dots. The polka-dotted pajama pattern is the most common found on Drowsy. A pull cord talker, Drowsy is 15 1/2 inches tall with a vinyl head and cloth body. Mattel reintroduced Drowsy in years 1974 and 2000. They advertised Drowsy as a cuddly nighttime friend who talks and says fun bedtime phrases. Drowsy is reissued as both a black or white cuddly doll wearing her polka-dotted pajamas. She originally said eleven phrases. The updated Drowsy says the five original phrases and in addition, when you lay her down she says, "Mommy, kiss me goodnight" and when the lights go out she says, "I go to sleep now. Night, night!"

Drowsy Reproduction. (Value I)

W. C. FIELDS

What's up my little chickadee? W.C. Fields is a cuddly stuffed talker. Who could resist his sense of humor, clever phrases and the wonderful character face with the big red nose? This 1966 pull cord talker, W.C. Fields, is dressed in his striped topcoat with hat and gloves. A red vest and pants make him a distinguished character. A flower boutonnière completes his dapper outfit to win the hearts of his best girl and children we knew he really loved. This stuffed talker will take you back to the humor and fun of W.C. Fields, a classic comic character.

W. C. Fields Stuffed Talker.
John & Frances Wiedey Collection (Value H)

BUFFY & MRS. BEASLEY

Buffy is the little girl from the familiar television program *Family Affair*. The TV show was popular from 1960 to 1971. Made by Mattel, she is all vinyl and is almost 11 inches tall. Buffy has painted eyes with freckles on her nose. Her rooted reddish blond hair is styled in a ponytail. She wears a red polka dot top with a red skirt. Buffy carries a 6 inch miniature Mrs. Beasley doll. Pull Buffy's talking ring and she says eight phrases. You never know what Buffy will say next.

Buffy & Mrs. Beasley. Roxanne Wallis Collection. (Value G)

Dr. Dolittle. Amelia Bubolz Collection. (Value G)

DR. DOLITTLE DOLL

Dr. Dolittle, played by Rex Harrison is a talking doll who introduces himself with "How do you do, I'm Doctor Dolittle," plus nine more phrases in star Rex Harrison's own voice. His top hat, coat and vest are removable. He stands 24 inches tall. An animal star Pushmi-Pullyu, the two-headed llama-type animal from the Doctor Dolittle movie is also a talker. Both talkers are made by Mattel.

Captain Kangaroo Advertising Records. Bruce Zeeman Collection. (Value I)

CAPTAIN KANGAROO RECORD

In the 1950s every girl and boy woke up to Captain Kangaroo. He shared adventures, sang songs and children marched around the breakfast table to the *Captain Kangaroo Marching Song!* This 1956 advertising record featured Captain Kangaroo, Buster Brown and Tige the dog. They were advertising the Buster Brown shoes; the shoes that every child wanted to wear while marching with Captain Kangaroo. This 4 1/2 inch 78 rpm record could be played on any child's phonograph of the day and was given away with the purchase of a pair of Buster Brown shoes. Captain Kangaroo songs were available on Columbia Records.

MONKEES TALKING HAND PUPPET

"Hey, Hey, we're the Monkees, and people say we monkey around!" The Monkees are pull-string talkers and singers! This doll puppet features the four members of the Monkees singing group. The puppet is circa 1966. The Monkees were a group put together by interviewing applicants for a screen test. The screen testes were measured by a computerized survey of a sample TV audience. The final four were Davy, Mike, Peter, and Micky, now known as The Monkees. Their first TV episode debuted on September 12, 1966 in full color. In 1967 it won an Emmy Award for Outstanding Comedy Series and Direction. These four guys, known as the Monkees spoke to their generation. They were good-natured boys who balanced fun with responsibility and always lent help to others. Two of their big song hits were *The Last Train to Clarksville* and *I'm A Believer.*

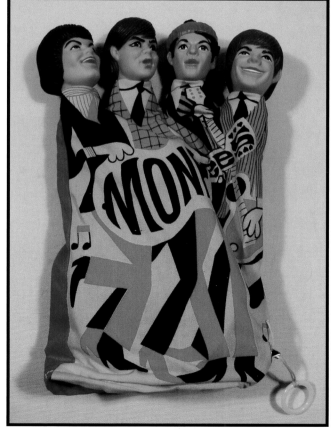

Monkees Talking Hand Puppet.
Amelia Bubolz Collection. (Value H)

Beatles Phonograph. Joe Hilton BeatleBay Collection. (Value D)

BEATLES PHONOGRAPH

It's Beatlemania! The four lads from Liverpool, England have captured the hearts of American teenagers. To play the songs of the fab four, George Harrison, John Lennon, Paul McCartney and Ringo Starr, they had their Beatles portable phonograph. The 1964 Beatles Record player was a must for every Beatle fan of the day. The phonograph was manufactured in the USA and licensed by NEMS Enterprises LTD. London. *Let Me Hold Your Hand; All My Loving; I Saw Her Standing There;* and *Twist and Shout* were played on this Beatles portable. Their songs sold millions, but this Beatles phonograph is rare. The Beatles were found on the inside lid and also on the outside of this fabulous phonograph. The phonograph could play 78, 45, 33 1/3, and 16 rpm speeds. It had a tone control, but for all Beatle lovers the sound was loud!

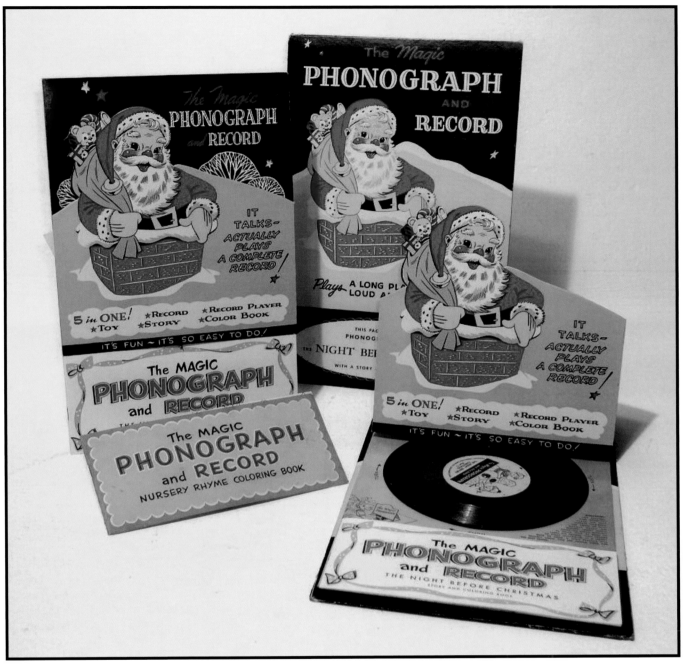

Magic Phonograph & Record. (Value I)

MAGIC PHONOGRAPH AND RECORD

Like magic this flat cardboard book transforms into a phonograph. It is the magic of Christmas and nursery rhymes all in one. A needle is attached to the edge of a sturdy cardboard standup card. The child would place the needle on the record and with a pencil turn the record and like magic it would play a song. It was five toys in one. It was a record player, record, toy, story, and coloring book all in one. These Magic Phonograph coloring books came in various themes. It was fun and easy to make the record play. It talked and actually played a complete record. It was magic!

MICKEY MOUSE PHONOGRAPH & RECORD SET

Every child of the 1950s & 1960s wanted to be a member of the Mickey Mouse Club. Mattel in cooperation with Walt Disney Productions issued this five record set. The 78 rpm records are 6 3/4 inches in size. As Roy Williams said: "Here's your very own Mickey Mouse Club. Inside this folder are colorful scenes from our TV show. And on the five new-process, non-breakable records you'll hear Roy Williams, Mickey Mouse, Donald Duck. And from the show too the records will play your Mickey Mouse Club March, the Mouseketeer Song and other musical favorites. With this Mattel Musical Map you can enjoy the Mickey Mouse Club anytime you want to...and entertain your friends with a show all your own. You can tell it's Mattel, it's swell."

Mickey Mouse Battery Record Player. (Value H)
Record Set. (Value G)

MICKEY MOUSE PHONOGRAPH

A Mickey Mouse battery operated phonograph was brought on the market by SHELCORE Inc. of N.J. in cooperation with Walt Disney Productions. This white plastic record player with Mickey on the lid could spin both 78 rpm and 45 rpm records. It was truly portable and made entirely of unbreakable plastic.

The Lionel Mickey Mouse Club Phonograph played 78 rpm tunes from the Mickey Mouse Club program for Mouseketeers to rally around wearing their Mouseketeer ears. The phonograph is electric with an acoustic reproducer. It was made by the famous Lionel Toy Company with the cooperation of Walt Disney Productions. This portable electric phonograph could be taken to Mickey Mouse Club meetings at friends homes as they had their own club meeting.

Mickey Mouse Phonograph by Lionel. (Value G)

MICKEY MOUSE CLUB RECORD

Join the Mickey Mouse Club on the Mouseketune's 33 1/3 record from 1975. In stereophonic sound you can hear special songs by Annette Funicello as well as exciting western songs from the "Triple R Ranch Adventures of Spin & Marty." The Mickey Mouse Club Opening March will have you marching around the breakfast table and wiggling your ears. Over half of the 21 Mouseketeer favorites were written by entertainer Jimmie Dodd.

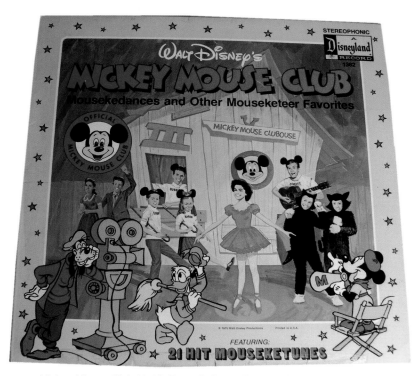

Mickey Mouse Club 33 1/3 Record. Bruce Zeeman Collection. (Value I)

BABES IN TOYLAND PHONOGRAPH

Babes In Toyland Phonograph. (Value G)

The Babes In Toyland drum phonograph is perfect to present fairy tale songs that remind tots of the musical, *Babes In Toyland.* The cardboard drum is 15 inches high and 14 inches in diameter. Just plug it in and insert a needle into the plastic reproducer and you are ready to enjoy songs and music. It was 1903 when *Babes in Toyland* was introduced. The music was by Victor Herbert. This musical was a venture to capitalize on the grand success of the *Wizard of Oz.* Disney released a theatrical version in 1961. Mouseketeer Annette Funicello, Ray Bolger and Ed Wynn appeared in a 1961 updated version of *Babes in Toyland.* It was a happy excursion into the world of Mother Goose. All roads led to the magical toy land as Mary Contrary and Tom Piper prepare for their wedding. The villain Barnaby wants Mary for himself and kidnaps Tom. The *March of the Wooden Soldiers* saves the day and Tom and Mary live happily ever after in Walt Disney's first musical production.

MICKEY MOUSE GENERAL ELECTRIC PHONOGRAPH

Mickey Mouse was creative in playing his 45 rpm records with his hands. The stylus is incorporated into this smart mouse's hand and his finger played the record. He greets his Mouseketeers with a big "Hi Kids!" on the inside of the cover. This phonograph model GE RP3122A was made by General Electric Company. This plastic phonograph is truly a 1960s toy with the aqua blue interior and Mickey wearing his matching bow tie and striped shirt. Disneyland records were provided for children to hear their favorite Disney characters tell a story and sing a song as children did the Mouseketeer march.

Mickey Mouse GE Phonograph. (Value H)

GENERAL ELECTRIC SHOW'N TELL PICTURESOUND

This 1964 General Electric Show'N Tell is both a phonograph and color slide viewer. It was the new media for kids. It plays a record while simultaneously playing a filmstrip and projecting it on a front viewing screen. Filmstrips and records were made specifically for this phonograph/viewer. The phonograph plays both 45 rpm and 33 1/3 rpm records. The Show'N Tell records have a storyboard filmstrip telling the story as the record plays. The filmstrip automatically feeds itself upward one frame at a time to go along with the music. The picturesound programs were both fun and educational. They had program libraries on *Fairy Tales and Cartoons, Children's Classics, History, Science and Space, The World We Live In* and *Steps to Knowledge*. Educational material was from the editors of Childcraft, The How and Why Library, and The World Book Encyclopedia.

Show' N Tell Phonograph and Viewer. (Value H)

Magic Talking Books. Dan Zeeman Collection. (Value I)

MAGIC TALKING BOOKS

Magic Talking Books are storybooks with a 78 rpm record on the front of the book. The entire book is placed over the turntable spindle of the phonograph. This makes it impossible to read the book while listening to the record. The little ones could either read the story and then listen to the record or treat themselves to the song and then decide to read the Magic Talking Book. These books were made by the John C. Winston Co. in 1955.

Cricket Record. (Value I)

CRICKET RECORDS

Cricket records were made in 1953 by the Pickwick Sales Corporation of N.Y. These unbreakable plastic records were a real hit with the kids. The record sleeves were well illustrated to the delight of any small child.

Look N Listen Records. (Value I)

LOOK N LISTEN RECORDS

Each record tells a fascinating story and lets the child hear the actual sounds of animals. Hear the lion roar or the bird sing a song. The records came in a 4 picture- record set with the interesting facts about the animals found on the back of the record. The real bird calls and stories were prepared in cooperation with the National Audubon Society. The records were registered in 1956 by the Universal Color Corp., N.Y.

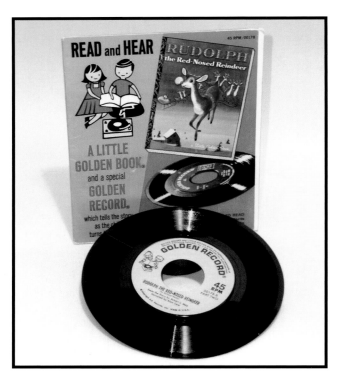

Golden Book Record Album. Gfell Family Collection. (Value I)

POPEYE LITTLE GOLDEN RECORD

That strong sailor man, Popeye recorded songs of health for the little ones. He sang *Lonely Tooth* and *Ah Choo!* Popeye's one health tip was to always eat your spinach to grow strong like Popeye and win Olive Oyl's favor. The songs were recorded by Jack Mercer and Mae Questel on a 45 rpm Golden record.

Marbleized Records . (Value I)

GOLDEN BOOK RECORD

Golden Records of New York promoted Read & Hear books and records for 69 cents. A Little Golden Book with a Golden Record of 1963, gave children the opportunity to learn and read as they listened to the record. Every word in the book is spoken on the recording. A special sound effect tells the child when to turn the page and when to turn the record over. They suggested that the child be allowed to play the phonograph so that they can hear the story and see the pictures and the words as many times as they like. The outstanding illustrations were by various artists and the Golden Record was unbreakable. On the back of the album cover it stated that parents will now be able to let the phonograph take over the job of reading "just one more."

Popeye Little Golden Record. (Value I)

MARBLEIZED RECORDS

Children's records were made to entertain, educate and catch the eye of the young record buyer. Marbleized records were very eye catching. The majority of children's records were of a solid color. It is rare to find these attractive rainbow colored records. The special marbleized records were made for children by Voco Inc. in 1949, and Happy Time Records, a Pickwick International Product, in 1962. These multicolored records are unique and added to the enchantment of record collecting by children of all ages.

HOWDY DOODY

"Hey kids. What time is it?" "It's Howdy Doody Time!" Anytime was Howdy Doody time when you had your very own Howdy Doody Phono Doodle player. Howdy Doody and Clarabell the clown are imprinted in red on the yellow plastic phonograph with the blue 78 rpm turntable and red tone arm. The records feature Howdy Doody and his creator "Buffalo" Bob Smith. Story and songs were by Edward Kean. Howdy and Bob Smith entertained and taught children of the 1950s the do's and don'ts and took them places and did exciting things together. These RCA Victor records are part of the Little Nipper Junior Series. The RCA Victor Company had a Little Nipper Record Club, which children could join. They received a membership card, Little Nipper pin and could enter contests. Most important, they would receive an update of the newest record releases. Little Nipper and Howdy Doody made a great team in promoting these unbreakable records.

Howdy Doody Phono Doodle. (Value G)

Howdy Doody Records. (Value I)

Howdy Doody Phono Doodle. Lowell Gearhart Collection. (Value F)

Hey kids, how about this Howdy Doody Phono Doodle electric portable. It was made by Shura-tone Products, Brooklyn, N.Y. Open the lid to this Phono Doodle and you see Howdy with his red hair and big grin. Howdy and his buddy Little Nipper were a great team. Little Nipper barked, "Hurry---hurry---to Howdy Doody's Laughing Circus. You'll see Girard the Giraffe, Herbie the Happy Hippo and Charlie the Chattering Chimp." This album was more fun than a barrel of monkeys! How about a ride with Howdy on his Air-O-Doodle. It was partly car and partly train---partly ship and partly plane. You could take a trip with Howdy as he rides over the candy rainbow and shares his trip on a 78 rpm record entitled Howdy Doody Air-O-Doodle.

It's Howdy Doody's Christmas Party. Everyone was invited including Buffalo Bob Smith, Clarabell the clown, Mr. Bluster, The Inspector, Oil Well Willie, The Flubabub, Dilly Dally, Princess Summerfall Winterspring and of course Santa Claus. Howdy's records were available at your favorite record store in the 78 rpm version or the new 45 rpm large hole records.

Howdy Doody's Christmas Party Record. Lowell Gearhart Collection. (Value I)

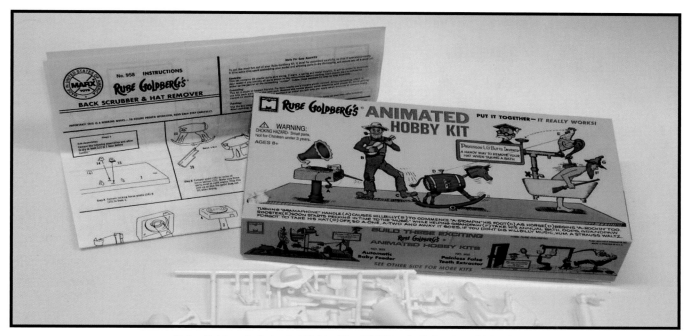

Rube Goldberg's Animated Hobby Kit. Gfell Family Collection. (Value I)

RUBE GOLDBERG HOBBY KIT

A Hobby Kit by Marx Toy Corp of 1965 had Rube Goldberg put together a back scrubber and hat remover all animated by an old fashioned horn gramophone. Children could follow the detailed instructions and be a Rube Goldberg. They were advertised as exciting animated hobby kits. Events started by: "turning the Gramaphone handle (A) causes Hillbilly (B) to commence a-stompin his foot (C) as horse (D) begins a-rockin too rooster (E) soon starts pecking in time to the music while helping grandpaw (F) take his annual bath, oops grandpaw forgot to take his hat (G) off so, a one, a two, and away it goes, if you don't dig hillbilly music, hum a Strauss waltz."

Hasbro Berliner Phonograph. (Value H)

HASBRO BERLINER PHONOGRAPH

Young inventors could relive the great moments of history and snap together a Berliner Phonograph. It was an authentic working replica. They learned about Berliner's original phonograph which established basic principles of sound reproduction. An enclosed booklet gave the history of the great inventor Emile Berliner. The completed replica played 45 RPM records. This phonograph was part of the Inventor Classic by Hasbro.

Sing-A-Song of Inventors Record. (Value I)

SING-A-SONG OF INVENTORS

To help students gain insight into the important inventors a record album entitled *SING-A-SONG OF INVENTORS* was released on the Records of Knowledge label. It was produced under the personal supervision of Metropolitan Opera Star Nanette Guilford. "The Happy Students" put the inventions and life of Thomas Alva Edison to song.

News Release Photo of the New Lionel Kits for 1962. Jeff & Tonya Young Collection. (Value I)

LIONEL PHONOGRAPH INVENTOR KIT

Young inventors in the1960s could reconstruct great moments in science with the Lionel Inventor Kits. They could make a tinfoil recording or build the electric lamp just as Thomas Alva Edison did. On the box they told children: "It worked for Edison in 1877. It works for you now. Demonstrate your invention at your school." The kit came complete with a needle stylus and tinfoil to make a child's first recording. A 6 1/2 inch plastic bust of the Wizard, Thomas A. Edison came with the kit.

Lionel Phonograph Inventor Kit. Ben Zeeman Collection. (Value H)

ADVERTISING RECORDS

"Ho! Ho! Ho!---from the land of the Jolly Green Giant." Tennessee Ernie Ford and his pea-pickers sang the Green Giant's and everybody's favorite folk songs. In 1963 the Jolly Green Giant's favorite songs included: *For He's a Jolly Green Giant; How the Jolly Green Giant Found His Song and almost lost his Ho! Ho! Ho!* plus *Good Things from the Garden.* This was all packaged and frozen on a seven inch 33 1/3 long play record.

Jolly Green Giant Advertising Record. (Value I)

Post Raisin Bran Advertising Records.
Bob & Wendie Coon Collection. (Value I)

Post's Raisin Bran issued these Toytime Records & Picture Books in the 1940s. They were from the Catalog of Music You Can Enjoy, 420 Lexington Ave., NY. To obtain these records of *The Golden Goose; William Tell;* and *AliBaba and the 40 Thieves*, children would send in box tops to get their free records. Other cereal companies adhered cut-out records to the side or back of boxes and thus a form of advertising evolved that continues into the twenty-first century when children receive free CD'S.

This record plays "Reach for Skippy" on a folding cardboard advertising phonograph. This was a promotional item for storeowners selling Skippy Peanut Butter. To play this personal message from Skippy, you placed a pencil in the hole found on the label of the record and turned the record slowly and steadily. This phonograph often found its way to the hands of children who enjoyed the novelty of the advertising phonograph with big news from Skippy Peanut Butter.

Skippy Peanut Butter Phonograph. William Zeeman Collection. (Value H)

Sound A Round Talking Puzzle. Bob & Wendie Coon Collection. (Value I)

Peter Pan Record. (Value I)

SOUND A ROUND TALKING PUZZLE

In 1968 children could put together a puzzle and with the magic Sound A Round tone arm could hear the story about the puzzle. No batteries are needed for this toy by Whiteman Western Publishing Co. of Racine, Wisconsin. The child places the magic tone arm and speaker on the record. The grooves are found on the outside of the puzzle. The record remains stationary and the reproducer is rotated with a steady hand around the record. It was two toys in one and fun for all as they learned about Fire Chief Frank and other pals.

PETER PAN RECORDS

For 25 cents plus tax children could buy Peter Pan Records. They were unbreakable with a bright red label. The record sleeve has a little Peter Pan playing his flute. This little guy is also found on the label of this 25 cent Peter Pan Record.

Little Nipper Game. Barbara & Joseph Regan Collection. (Value G)

LITTLE NIPPER GAME & PIN

Members of the Little Nipper Club received an extra special gift from Little Nipper for Christmas. It was RCA Victor's Little Nipper Game. Five little nippers could play this game. First they had to push out one round Nipper marker for each player. Next they would spin the arrow for directions on where to go on the game board. When the player lands on a spot with directions he must obey them. First to reach Santa wins the game! On their way to visit Santa they would visit Roy Rogers, the witch from Snow White, Captain Hook, Spike Jones, the wolf from Little Red Riding Hood, Howdy Doody and many more of their favorite recording artist and storybook characters. The backside of the game advertised the new RCA Victor Kiddy Albums. Members of the Little Nipper Club would also receive a Little Nipper pin proclaiming them a Little Nipper Club Member.

Little Nipper Club Pin. (Value H)

RCA Train Children's Record Display. Lowell Gearhart Collection. (Value F)

"The Children's Music House" Record Album Display.
Diane & Kurt Nauck Collection. (Value D)

RCA CHILDREN'S RECORD DISPLAYS

Little Nipper rode in the "45 EP" Line train display to promote RCA Victor children's albums. The red train with the friendly conductor and Little Nipper is fifteen inches long and twelve and one half inches high. Up to 15 minutes of fun were found on each "45 Extended Play" album as they were displayed in the front box of the Little Nipper train.

"The Children's Music House" is an awesome RCA Victor dealer store display. The display is approximately five feet long, six feet high and three feet wide. This RCA Victor record display would be a real eye catcher for customers. It would display the many children's record albums sold by the RCA Victor Company. The Candy Land graphics on the cart are identical on both sides. It rolls on the RCA Victor wheels while Nipper is peering out the window.

CHAPTER 4

THE DISCO DECADE

It's the 1970s and 1980s. Disco Fever hit the continent. The Chatty Cathy doll has friends such as Cynthia in her hot pink dress, Chatty Patty and talking Baby Beans. Flip Wilson is making us laugh. Rodney Rippy doll tells us "Take Life a Little Easier." We have just a small representation of the dolls of the 1970s and 1980s in this chapter as books dedicated to talking dolls of this era have been printed for doll lovers of the disco years. Both boys and girls love sports, games, pop music and dolls that represent their entertainment idols. New sound technology of the day brings realism to toys of the disco years.

BUGS BUNNY PHONOGRAPH

It's disco rabbit and a 1970s Bugs Bunny "What's Up Doc" battery operated phonograph in disco colors of orange and green. This portable phonograph plays 33 1/3 and 45's. The phonograph is a "Big Sounder" as the record title on the cover of the phonograph exclaims. You can take it anywhere and chase those bunny rabbits while you play your favorite disco tune.

Bugs Bunny Phonograph. (Value G)

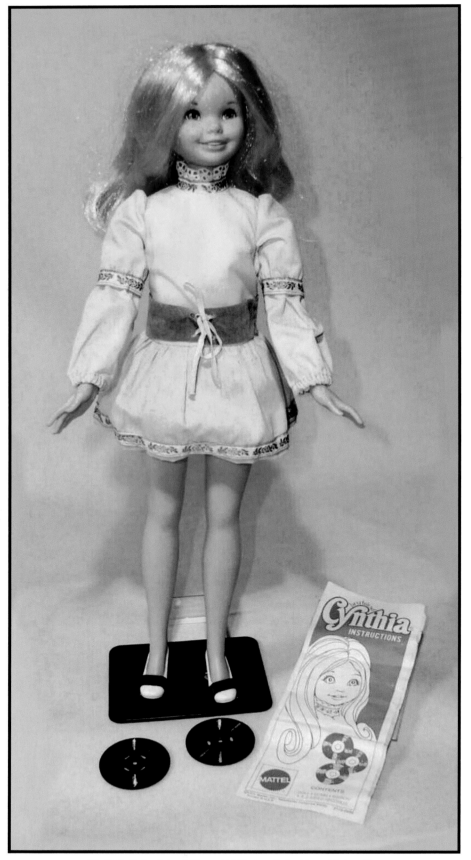

Cynthia Doll. John & Frances Wiedey Collection. (Value G)

CYNTHIA

Chatty Cathy returned in 1970. The Mattel Company made her much smaller. She did not resemble the original Chatty Cathy. She now has painted eyes and her hair is blond with a blue hair clip. She still had her freckles, but this Chatty reissue was as popular as the original. One reason could be she came with only one dress style. With a pull of her talking ring Chatty could talk, sing and whisper just as her original sister of the 1950s. Mattel issued many talking dolls in the 1970s and 1980s. The Cynthia doll is the super sized Barbie doll of 1972 introduced by Mattel. She is 19 inches tall and wears a hot pink mini dress. She plays small records that were black and also in various hot colors. Six records were available for the doll made by the Mattel Toy Company. Cynthia and Charmin' Chatty are the only two Mattel talking dolls to have changeable records. The records are inserted into a slot found on the doll's side. The common titles of the records feature indoor and outdoor fun activities. She is battery operated. Cynthia will talk when the button in the center of her back is pushed. She is made in Hong Kong. Other dolls introduced in the 1970s by Mattel were Timey Tell, Talking Twosome, Peachy, Mork, Talking Brad, Snow White, Bozo, Cat in the Hat, Teachy Talk, Mother Goose, and Myrtle from *My Three Sons* TV series. Mattel was a leader in making talking dolls for youngsters of the disco decade.

BABY TENDER LOVE

This baby doll is a soft rubber, and is a Baby Tender Love with her baby face, rosy cheeks and short blond hair. Just 16 inches tall, she was made from 1970 to 1973 by Mattel Toys.

Her bright pink bow in the back of her head is the pull cord that makes Baby Tender Love talk. She says several tender phrases, such as, "Peek-a-boo," "Ha Ha," "I'se a good girl," "Go bye-bye now" and "Knock, knock, mommy." Baby Tender Love drinks and wets. You can also purchase a Baby Tender Love paper doll book, authorized by Whitman Books in 1971.

Baby Tender Love. John & Frances Wiedey Collection.
(Value I)

CHATTY PATTY

Chatty Patty is the last Chatty doll added to the Chatty line of Mattel dolls in 1983. She was a white doll with blond hair or a black doll with black hair. She wears her pink outfit trimmed with lace and matching pink shoes. This 16 1/2 inch doll was a smart little girl. She knows which toy she is holding and talks about it! She says up to ten things. Pull her talking ring and she talks about her puppy and about her present too! She talks about her mirror, comb and brush and she talks without her toys as well.

Chatty Patty Doll. Robin & Joan Rolfs Collection. (Value H)

STUFFED DOLLS

Flip Wilson was the TV character that exclaimed "What you see is what you get, honey," and "Easy on my String." Shindana Toys introduced Flip with the flip side Geraldine doll in 1970. His voice box is Mattel.

Flip Wilson & Geraldine Doll.
John & Frances Wiedey Collection. (Value G)

Baby Beans. John & Frances Wiedey Collection. (Value H)

Cute little Baby Beans is a Mattel Toy and a J.C. Penney exclusive. She says eight phrases and is dressed in blue and pink pajamas with a matching nightcap. Her bean shaped face tells the story of her name "Baby Beans."

The lovable Hug Me Doll is made in Taiwan by Mattel, Inc. Press her "Hug Me" tag on her tummy and she says: "Stop, that tickles," "I'm hungry," "I want to play," "please rock me to sleep mommy," "mommy hug baby," "go night, night," and "please rock me to sleep."

Hug Me Doll. John & Frances Wiedey Collection. (Value I)

PEEWEE HERMAN

This comic celebrity doll is very popular. Perhaps it was his squeaky voice or his dapper red tie, white shirt, gray suit and white shoes. PeeWee is a "Matchbox" toy from 1987. He is a pull cord talker and measures 18 inches tall. PeeWee has a vinyl head, hands and feet with a cloth body.

PeeWee Doll with Pull Cord Talker.
Bessie & Floyd Seiter Collection. (Value I)

ERNEST

"Hey Vern, I'm Ernest." Ernest was a popular spokesperson for car sales and more. With that voice and toothy grin, Ernest got your attention. He says, "Hey Vern, I talk." Pull his cord and see what deals Ernest has for you. Made by Kenner in 1989 he proves how popular television commercials were in the 1970s and 1980s.

Ernest Doll. John & Frances Wiedey Collection. (Value I)

Give your daughter a daughter.

Give her Smartypants.™ She's more than just another talking doll. She answers questions.

Smartypants can tell mommy how many toes she has. And tell her which hand she's touching. Smartypants laughs when mommy tickles her.

And asks mommy to hold her tighter when she's being cuddled. Best of all, when mommy kisses Smartypants and tells her she loves her, Smartypants answers: "I love you too, mommy." Smartypants. She's more than just a doll. She's a daughter for your daughter.

Smartypants...by Topper.

© 1971 –Topper Corp., Elizabeth, N.J.

Smarty Pants Doll. (Value I)

SMARTY PANTS

Smarty Pants was a Topper Toy of 1971. Smarty Pants is more than just another talking doll. She answers questions. She can tell you how many toes she has, which hand you are touching and laughs when tickled. She is truly an 18 inch talker that deserves the name "Smarty Pants."

Crying Baby. John & Frances Wiedey Collection. (Value G)

CRYING BABY & PHONOGRAPH MUSIC BOX

This Crying Baby Doll is made in West Germany. She is 19 inches long and plays small colorful records. Her cloth body has a zipper, which opens in the back and exposes a plastic phonograph with interchangeable records. To change records, hold back the transmission plate and carefully pull the record from the center piece. Turn the record over or exchange the record. Press the record tightly on the plate. The speed adjustment is a white screw inside the box. The record will automatically stop when the cycle is finished. The mechanism is battery operated and marked "Minifon Made In Italy." Her records speak English. The voice or voices on the record are clear and childlike.

A wooden Schmid phonograph/music box plays *Those were the Days*. It is made of wood. The birds add a clever touch to this small 3 inch replica.

Schmid Wood Phonograph.
Julie Zeeman Collection. (Value I)

Gabbigale Doll. Robin & Joan Rolfs Collection. (Value H)

GABBIGALE

Kenner Toy Company made this smiling, talking doll in 1972. Her name is Gabbigale and she repeats everything a little girl would say to her. She is a hard plastic and vinyl doll with rooted blond hair and blue painted eyes. She has a battery operated recording mechanism to repeat your phrases. Raise her arm and pull her string to record your own message. Put her arm down and pull the string to hear her repeat what you said. She came in a bright red box. On the box it shows Gabbigale in her blue jumper outfit with a red print blouse. Red shoes complete her outfit. The red flower pull cord is pulled to record your message. Gabbigale will say everything you tell her to say!

INSTANT REPLAY RECORD MINIATURES

Football, racing and fast airplanes, what more could a boy or girl want? Mattel produced a collector series of 2 1/4 inch records that could be played in the Offense record player. You could have an instant replay of great sports events like Bart Starr throwing that touchdown pass for the Green Bay Packers or Willy Mays hitting that winning home run. Sports fans could also have instant replays of a Gold Cup Hydroplane, Bonneville Jet Car, Phantom Jets, the P-51 Jet or a Formula 1 Race car. The event was pictured on one side of the record and the record grooves found on the backside recorded the great sports event to be played again and again on instant replay.

Instant Replay Record Miniatures. (Value G)

FOOTBALL GAME

"Hear it Happen" was a talking football game by Mattel Inc., and marketed for football fans of all ages. Place the small record in the compact phonograph that came with the game, follow the play and you could be the quarterback that wins the game. This game came complete with a playing field, goalposts and scoreboard. The small records were placed in record racks during playtime. It was the talking football game of 1972.

"Hear It Happen Game" Talking Football Game. Brian Coon Collection. (Value G)

TALKING PICTURES SCHOOLHOUSE

In 1972 Mattel also introduced Preschool Talking Pictures Schoolhouse for pre-school children three to five years of age. It came complete with a parent guide. The child inserted the small picture record in the schoolhouse and learned about *Me, My Feeling and Manners*. This talking toy was safety tested and prepared the little tykes for the real schoolhouse.

Talking Pictures Schoolhouse. Justin Coon Collection. (Value I)

SOUNDWAGON

This Musical Toy Soundwagon travels around the grooves of a 33 1/3 record. The stylus of the Soundwagon tracks the grooves of the record as the truck speeds around the circular course of the stationary record. This musical toy is battery operated. The manufacturer warned that your record must be flat or the Soundwagon will travel around the record at an irregular speed. The wheels of the Soundwagon needed to be kept clean for proper traction. You could wipe the wheels with a cloth moistened with denatured alcohol from time to time. The sound wagons came in various colors and different logos could be found on the side of the Volkswagen bus.

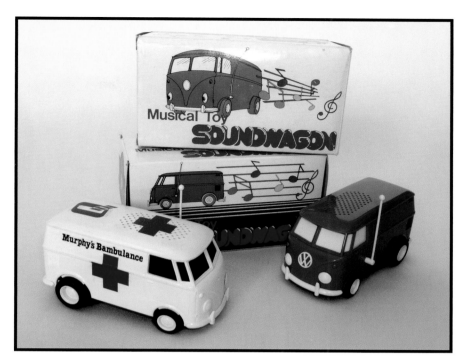

Two Different Models of the Soundwagon. (Value G)

Hokie Pokie Sound Machine and Record.
Ben Zeeman Collection. (Value H)

HOKIE POKIE SOUND MACHINE

A newer version of the Soundwagon returned in 1992. It was called the Hokie Pokie Sound Machine made by Angel Blue Inc., Blandon, Pa. It works on the exact same concept as the Soundwagon. Put this truck on a 33 1/3 record and around it would go to the amazement of the partygoers.

A special "Party Picture Disc" called the Hokie Pokie came with the 1992 version of the Soundwagon. On one side of the disc were tunes such as: *Mony-Mony, O'Happy Day* and *Blue Moon*. On the backside of the record were the operating instructions. Put the Hokie Pokie Sound Machine on the record and you could dance the Hokie Pokie!

Advertising Pop Records of the 1970s - 1980s. Bob & Wendie Coon Collection. (Value I)

ADVERTISING POP RECORDS

Dance to the disco beat of the Jackson Five, Bobby Sherman, the Monkees and The Archies. Fast food was the rage and you could sing the song *Potato Chip* as you ate your Big Mac. Many of these 33 1/3 small 7 inch records were give away premiums on cereal boxes and other tasty foods of the 1980s. The Pepsi Cola Company gave away a Superman record to promote their cool soft drink of the 1970s.

CHILDREN'S RECORDS

Children could purchase the songs from their favorite Walt Disney movies to hear over and over again. The Disneyland Vista Records dated 1977 gave children a head start in learning to read as they enjoyed the original soundtracks of their favorite movies. Mary Poppins sang her way into the hearts of children and they could hear the many songs from the film. Both 33 1/3 and 45 rpm recordings were available. Winnie the Pooh is still popular as Walt Disney tells the story of *Winnie the Pooh and the Blustery Day*. They could see the pictures, hear the record and read the book.

Disneyland Records. Gfell Family Collection. (Value I)

Gremlin Records. Gfell Family Collection. (Value I)

The Gremlins have arrived in the 1980s. A five set series of the Gremlins was produced in 1984 by Buena Vista Records of Burbank, California. A 33 1/3 record and storybook told the story of these lovable creatures and their adventures and escapes.

World's Smallest Victrola. William Zeeman Collection. (Value H)

SMALL TOY VICTROLAS

Mom, dad and the entire family could take a trip down memory lane. This 1983 miniature Victrola measured just 2 1/4 inches square at the base and 5 1/2 inches to the top of the horn. It plays 2 inch records and is powered by a 1.5 volt penlight battery.   Just like the real Victrola, you could hear distortion in the very high and low range. It was made by Poynter Products, Inc., Cincinnati, Ohio and came with six hit records of yesterday.

For children ages ten and up Woodkrafter Kits of Yarmouth, Maine made a Record Player Kit in 1987. It was part of a Science-Kraft-Series designed by Kyle Wickware.   The young inventor could build a finger powered record player, learn about sound vibrations and discover the world of physical science.

Woodkrafter Record Player Kit. Dan Zeeman Collection. (Value I)

CABBAGE PATCH TALKING KIDS

Cabbage Patch Talking Kids were born September, 1987. The Coleco Company claimed they utilized "an advanced microprocessor system," the most sophisticated technology being used in the doll industry. They responded to voice, touch and movement. Their elaborate vocabulary is unpredictable and includes small talk, talking between each other and singing. Special drinking cups that made drinking sounds were specially made for the Cabbage Patch Kids.

Cabbage Patch Talking Kids. Roxanne Wallis Collection. (Value G)

CABBAGE PATCH PHONOGRAPH

The Cabbage Patch Kid doll was a hit with the kids of the 1980s. Parents stood in line at toy stores to buy this doll that came with an original birth certificate. Cabbage Patch Kids is a trademark of and licensed from Original Appalachian Artwork Inc., Cleveland, Georgia, USA. The Cabbage Patch record player had the Cabbage Patch Kid flying amidst her favorite records and playing with the beautiful notes. It played both 45 and 33 1/3 rpm records. This phonograph was made by Original Artworks Inc.

Cabbage Patch Phonograph. (Value H)

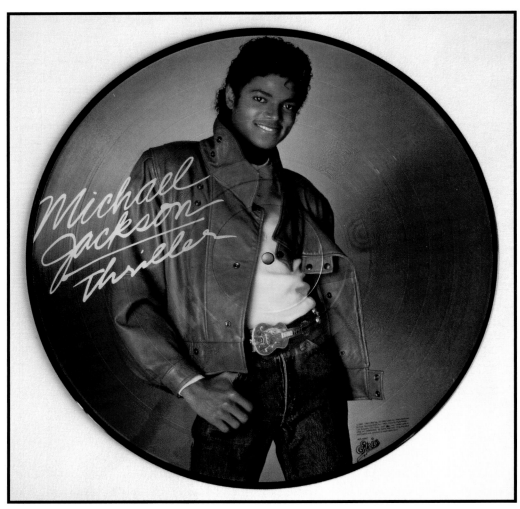

Thriller Picture Disc. (Value I) Thriller Viewmaster Reel & Record. (Value I)

MICHAEL JACKSON THRILLER

Teenagers of the 1980s were thrilled with the moves and songs of Michael Jackson. He was the teenage idol of the day. Michael could be seen as well as heard on the Viewmaster stereo reel. Michael Jackson's *Thriller* is the best selling album of all time. 45 million copies of the *Thriller* album were sold worldwide. The 1982 album won eight Grammy Awards.

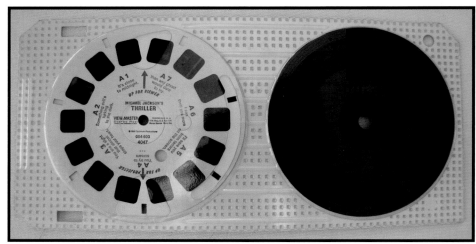

Michael Jackson Vanity Fair Record Player. (Value I)

Teens can dance to 45 and 33 1/3 rpm Michael Jackson records on this portable record player with Michael Jackson's signature. Michael Jackson, the youngest member of the Jackson Five was a child performer who became unquestionably the biggest pop star of the 1980s.   His famous moonwalk and instantly identifiable voice, eye popping dance moves and musical versatility brought him to stardom as he dominated the music charts. His 1982 album *Thriller* became the biggest-selling album of all time and is probably his best-known accomplishment. He is also the first black artist to find stardom on MTV, breaking down the boundaries of race and making music videos an art form.

PIONEER PHONOGRAPH

The Pioneer round compact plastic phonograph was portable to take to any party. It had the technology of the day. This "Pioneer Hawaiian" phonograph was labeled "For Junior Use." It requires six "C" size batteries to operate. The 3 3/4 inch diameter turntable played both 33 1/3 and 45 rpm records with the included adaptor. Electronics included no visible amplifier circuit. The output was generated by a unique high output cartridge. This compact plastic phonograph was made in Japan.

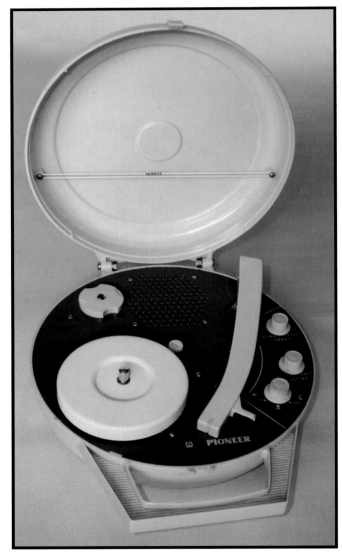

Pioneer Phonograph.
Bob & Wendie Coon Collection. (Value I)

FISHER PRICE RECORD PLAYER

This Fisher Price Phonograph of the 1970s is one of the most durable phonographs for children. It comes with five plastic records in various colors. It is called a music box record player because the records are like music box discs. The musical movement was made in Switzerland. The child learns how to put a record on a phonograph, put the tone arm on the record and enjoy music. This toy is a great way to teach young children about playing old phonograph records.

Fisher Price Phonograph. Pat Zeeman Collection. (Value I)

The Fox and the Hound Read Along Book and Tape.   (Value I)

BOOKS AND TAPES

Read-Along Book cassettes were a new technology that allowed children to see the pictures, hear the tape and read the book. Each book and cassette combination is a fun-filled experience in music and story adventure. The book is twenty-four pages filled with full-color illustrations and comes with a high quality read-along cassette. Disneyland Vista Records and Tapes of Burbank, California produced many of the popular read-along books and tape cassette books of the 1970s.

Kid Stuff Record. Wayne Singer Collection. (Value I)

KID STUFF RECORDS

All your favorite characters, stories and songs could be found on the 1970s & 1980s Kid Stuff long-playing records and tapes, book and tape sets, and book and record sets. Pac-Man, Bugs Bunny, Benji, Care Bears, Fat Albert, Barbie, Rocky, Master of the Universe, Pink Panther, Strawberry Shortcake and the Dukes of Hazzard could be found on Kid Stuff. Kid Stuff talking storybooks were an entertaining way to encourage children to read. They could see the pictures, hear the story and read the book. Kid Stuff records and tapes were a division of I.J.E. Inc., Hollywood, Florida.

Picture Records. Becky Singer Collection. (Value I)

PICTURE RECORDS

Picture records are the rage of the 1980s. Pac-Man, Snow White and Strawberry Shortcake were just a few collectors' series that every child wanted. Pac-Man was not only on the computer, but on the turntable as well. These 12 inch 33 1/3 rpm records were available from the American Greetings Corp., Kid Stuff Records. The Kid Stuff Phonograph Picture Disc was in a Limited Edition Collector series. They took children to the magic kingdom and magic lands of all the favorite characters of the 1980s.

Disney's "Main Street Electrical Parade" would have had Thomas Edison beaming with pride as over a half million colorful lights re-create classic scenes from Disney's best loved films. The sounds of the parade were captured on a 33 1/3 seven inch picture record. Songs such as: *Electric Fanfare, Cinderella, Brazzle Dazzle Day, Whistle While You Work* and *The Mickey Mouse March* are some of the selections from Disney's "Main Street Electrical Parade."

Disney's Main Street Electrical Parade Record. (Value I)

4-20

Mickey & Minnie Mouse Phonograph. Robin & Joan Rolfs Collection. (Value G)

MICKEY AND FRIENDS

Mickey Mouse is still popular with the Disco generation. In 1976 a 6 inch plastic talking Mickey was still winning the hearts of children. This plastic mouse with the big ears chatted to the kids and made their dreams come true at Disneyland. Talking Mickey was made by Mattel Inc. Mouseketter's can dance with Mickey, Minnie and Pluto to the latest 45 and 78 rpm hits on this two speed portable by the Porter Spear Co. The enclosed record order form lists twenty-three 6 inch 78 rpm records and fourteen 45 rpm records available from the Spears Products Co, Orange, N.J. Walt Disney Productions provided a colorful graphic for the inside lid of this otherwise utilitarian electrically driven acoustic phonograph. The price sticker from a Target Department Store indicates that it sold for $8.97.

Amelia Bubolz Collection. (Value G)

Storytime Jukebox. Bill Klinger Collection. (Value G)

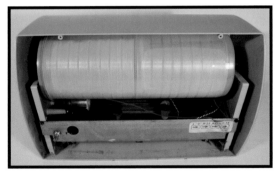

Storytime Jukebox Back.

STORYTIME JUKEBOX

The colors are disco green and pink. The children can select their favorite story from this Storytime Jukebox by Kenner. The amazing thing about this 1971 toy is that it plays a 16 track cylinder record made of plastic. Moreover, the grooves are vertically modulated. Imagine, in the 1970s the grooves on this cylinder record are in the same manner that Thomas A. Edison recorded songs on wax cylinders over 90 years earlier! It is also powered by batteries, not unlike the first commercial phonograph. A bright pink paper liner was inserted into the cylinder to add a bright Lambert pink color.

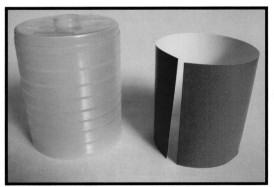

Cylinder Showing Pink Liner.

Storytime Cylinder.

4-22

CHAPTER 5

THE COMPUTER GENERATION

The computer chip represents a new means of sound reproduction. It is not a phonograph that reproduces sound vibrations etched in a groove. Rather, the digital electronic medium records sounds as binary digits that represent the frequency and intensity of the sound signal. It takes little space and does not need to be cranked or pulled. At the push of a button or simply by talking to the toy, the sound-activated computer chip will "talk" to the child. It is a new age of toys. These dolls and toys have become more outspoken. Phrases like: "Don't have a Cow Man" or "You got it Dude" and "No Way Jose!" are typical expressions of the modern day. Some dolls even have a built-in attitude. On a progressive note, many dolls are multicultural and can sing and talk in any language. Today's toys are not powered by the child's imagination, but by an interactive computer chip. Children have a voice activated pet called Neopets. The Neopet changes its mood at the tone of the child's voice. There are fashion diva's who talk about a girl's favorite subject, what to wear. Pop dreamer dolls can rock like a pop star and even jam with their fellow pop dreamer dolls. Annabelle and Baby Chou Chou are like real babies. They cry, their lips move as they enjoy their bottle. Annabelle will either wake up laughing or crying. Don't worry if she is crying, just pat her on the back and she will calm down.

BARBIE

Barbie is one of the most popular dolls of the twentieth century. The Mattel Barbie of 1991 talked. Press the button on her back and she chatted about all the things girls liked best. There are many talking Barbie dolls as well as her boyfriend Ken and their many friends. Entire books are dedicated to the famous Barbie doll.

Teen Talk Barbie Doll. Becky Singer Collection. (Value H)

Reproduction Chatty Cathy's . Frances Wiedey Collection. (Value H)

CHATTY CATHY

Chatty Cathy returned as a reissued doll in 1998. She is almost like the first nineteen inch Chatty Cathy. Each doll is numbered and comes with a Certificate of Authenticity. In 1999 Chatty Cathy was reissued as a J.C. Penney Exclusive. A 1999 Holiday Chatty Cathy was also made. She is dressed for the Christmas holidays in her red and plaid jumper with white blouse. All the 1998-1999 Chatty Cathy dolls have the same mechanism as the original Chatty Cathy of 1959. A pull string activates a permanent record. In the years 2001 and 2002 smaller 15 inch reproduction Chatty Cathy dolls were issued. Chatty still wears her original blue dress, but lacks her original freckles and detail. However, this time she has a computer sound chip. If this mechanism breaks, there are no replacement parts for repair. The chip is encoded with the voice of actress June Foray who was the voice for the original Chatty Cathy.

MICHELLE

Michelle was the little talking girl in the television series "Full House." She was introduced to her fans in 1991. A 15 inch Michelle has vinyl arms, legs and head. She has a soft cuddly body. Her bright blue eyes are painted and a smile shows a row of white teeth. She has her ponytail and loves to wear jeans. She is quite outspoken! She says the phrases of the 1990's like: "Whoa Baby," "You got it dude," "Don't call me squirt," "No way Jose!," "My name is Michelle," and "Are you talking to me?" The dolls are now talking back to us and demanding our attention. Times have changed!

Michelle Doll.
Bessie & Floyd Seiter Collection. (Value H)

Mrs. Beasley Reproduction. John & Frances Wiedey Collection. (Value H)

MRS. BEASLEY

Mrs. Beasley is Buffy's granny doll from the television show *Family Affair*. Mrs. Beasley was always ready with a kind word. The 22 inch pull cord talker Mrs. Beasley doll was introduced in 1966. In 1967 Mrs. Beasley was sold in a completely sealed box that did not have a window to watch Buffy and her friends play. She said the same phrases as the earlier Mrs. Beasley. The newest Mrs. Beasley has the voice of Cheryl Ladd with eleven sayings for Buffy and her friends. She was sold by the Ashton Drake Company in the year 2000.

WOODY

"Howdy partner!" It's Woody, the star of Disney's *Toy Story*. He is a pull string doll, ready to entertain a child at a moment's notice and tell them that, "You're my favorite deputy!" He was manufactured by Thinkway Toys.

TALKING WALDO

Where's Waldo? Wow! Pow! Waldo can talk! Insert the disc and you can hear Waldo say twenty clever things. This Waldo Doll came with two discs and was made by the Mattel Toy Company.

Woody Doll. (Value I)

Talking Waldo in Box. John & Frances Wiedey Collection. (Value H)

Comes to Life Interactive Books. Bob & Wendie Coon Collection. (Value I)

COMES TO LIFE INTERACTIVE BOOKS

Each page of these books comes to life with the help of the Storyplayer. A small record is found on each page. Put the Storyplayer on the record and hear sounds from the story being read. This interactive book is by Yes! Entertainment Corporation of Pleasanton, CA.

MINIATURE PHONOGRAPH

This tiny one inch phonograph winds up and scoots across the playroom. The bright orange phonograph with a smiley face with the yellow horn spins in circles to the delight of the child. Made in Singapore it brings a smile to the face of any boy or girl.

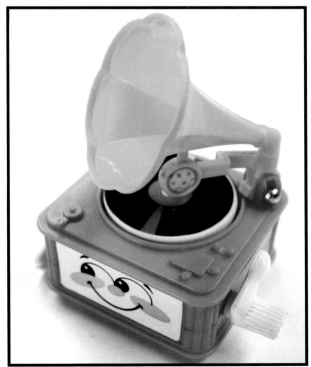

Miniature Plastic Phonograph.
Ron & Janet Keuler Collection. (Value I)

Neopets Scorchio & Grarrl. Austin Singer & Dylan Singer Collection. (Value I)

NEOPETS

Neopets are a voice activated pet. They can be a child's best friend. The Neopets count on their owners to keep them happy and playful as their mood changes. The Neopet comes alive at the sound of the child's voice. It responds to the tone of your voice with sound, movements and lights. The Neopet changes its voice depending upon your mood. It makes over twenty-seven sounds including laughs and giggles. It knows when it's being picked up and put down and reacts with happy sounds and actions. "Scorchios are outgoing and friendly most of the time. They prefer hot climates, especially the deserts and volcanic regions of Neopia. Grarrls are ferocious creatures or at least they try to be. With lots of care and attention, Grarrls can grow to be some of the strongest Neopians." There are many Neopets to collect such as Usul, Acara, Ixi, Gelert, Kougra, Kacheek, Mynci, Uni and Shoyru to name a few. Neopets are a thinking toy made by Thinkway Toys. You can visit the Neopets website at: www.neopets.com

CAILLOU

Caillou is one of the PBS kids. Press his tummy and he talks. He is dressed as the kid of 2003 with baggy pants, T-shirt and wearing his cap backwards. Caillou is soft and cuddly. Caillou speaks ten different phrases. He stands 15 inches tall. Caillou is a preschooler's best friend. He comes with his own storybook. The child can read the book and then press his tummy for a verbal response. He works on two "AA" batteries. Caillou is made by Irwin Toy Ltd., Niagara Falls, New York.

Caillou. (Value I)

Nikki Fashion Diva. (Value I)

NIKKI FASHION DIVA

Nikki is the ultimate fashion diva of year 2004. Push the top of her head and her lips light up and she talks fashion with you. She wears the platform shoes for the techno tall height. Nikki is a real fashion diva made by the Mattel Company. There are five fashion Diva's: Alexa, Tia, Nikki, Miranda, and Summer.

GABRIELLE POP DREAMER

Gabrielle is a 10 1/2 inch interactive pop dreamer with clothes and guitar computer chip recognition. Gabrielle is a Radio Disney Pop Dreamer. She has a real personality. She may seem like the quiet type until she starts talking about two of her favorite things: singing and reading. She talks, sings songs and plays guitar. Little girls can rock like a pop star and dream like a princess with Gabrielle. She really can rock the house in her amber pants! You can share Gabrielle's wardrobe with other pop dreamer dolls. When you dress her up she tells you what she thinks about her outfit. She will even tell you if she is wearing one of her friend's outfits. Together with her friends Ella and Ari they can jam in pairs or sing in a trio. Each one of these dolls is ready to rock like a pop star and dream like a princess. This Disney toy is made by Thinkway Toys, New York.

Gabrielle Pop Dreamer. (Value I)

LIZZIE LANGUAGE LITTLES

Toys connect the children of the world and Language Littles dolls connect the world one word at a time. They are a fun way to learn how to speak phrases in another language. Lizzie speaks Spanish and English. Jolie speaks French and English, Sophie speaks Italian and English, and Ling speaks Chinese and English. The dolls are 14 inches tall, soft and dressed in the fashions of the day for children. Their hair is a soft yarn and is in the latest style. Just press their hand and you will learn a new language, gain a new friend and have a better understanding of children from all over the world. They require three "AA" batteries. They are made by Language Littles, New York and manufactured in China.

Lizzie Language Littles. (Value I)

Tigger. Toysrus, Appleton, WI. (Value I)

GET UP'N BOUNCE TIGGER

Get up and do *The Bounce* with Tigger. Children can dance the *Whoop-de-Dooper Bounce* song. This bouncing Tigger is an active toy. He really gets into his dance! He has arms that kids can move and pose. Tigger is based on the *Winnie the Pooh* works by A. A. Milne and E. H. Shepard. The *Whoop-de-Dooper Bounce*, has words and music by Richard M. Sherman and Robert B. Sherman, Wonderland Music Company Inc. You can really get your exercise with this 12 1/2 inch Tigger. Tigger stands up, dances, sings, bounces, and sits down all by himself. You never know what he will do next. Tigger's cool sound effects and silly phrases add to the fun! Tigger is made by Fisher-Price Toys and is manufactured in China.

Princess Belle Doll. Toysrus, Appleton Wisconsin.   (Value H)

PRINCESS BELLE

Princess Belle can reenact Disney's story of *Beauty and the Beast*. She is a 14 inch tall interactive doll. She can dance, sing and as she arrives at the castle, she can trigger ticking clocks, creaking doors and other sound effects. The castle's residents can be placed in her right hand to talk to her. Lumiere guides her way, Mrs. Potts offers encouragement and Cogsworth makes sure Belle is on time to the ball. She comes with a yellow and blue gown. She may hold an interactive mirror with pictures of the beast, the prince and the rose, a hairbrush to use on Bell's long brown hair. A locket and other small accessories come with Princess Belle. She is a Disney princess and has the original voice from Disney's *Beauty and the Beast*. Three "AAA" batteries are required to operate Princess Belle. My Interactive Princess Belle is made by Playmates Toy Inc. of Costa Mesa, CA.

Magic*Mates Cinderella. (Value I)

MAGIC*MATES CINDERELLA

Cinderella is a Disney Magic*Mates voice activated doll. She stands 4 1/2 inches tall. Cinderella has over eighteen sayings. Cinderella sways and dances back and forth as her arms move up and down and her dress lights up. You can collect an entire set of Disney Magic*Mates like Belle, Ariel, Simba, Buzz Lightyear and Pooh. These tiny Magic*Mates know when they are being lifted up or put down. They react with voice, movement and light. They are manufactured by Thinkway Toys, New York and are made in China.

PRINCESS MAGIC WAND

A little girl cannot be a princess without her magic wand. With the wave of this 14 inch interactive Disney Princess Magic Wand, every little girl can make a wish. Wave the wand, press the button and magically a favorite Disney Princess will light up and talk to her. Children can hear Cinderella, Belle, or Snow White make their wishes come true. The Interactive Magic Wand is manufactured by Thinkway Toys, New York and is made in China.

Disney Princess Magic Wand.
(Value I)

DORA THE EXPLORER

Cowgirl Dora explores the open range with her trusty pony Pinto. Press Dora's left boot to hear her sing and say phrases as she rides along. Press her boot again to hear Pinto the Pony join in the song. She sings galloping, galloping here we go, which is a catchy song that children can sing along. "Eee Haww!" Dora speaks both English and Spanish. Dora has many other friends that also go exploring the world. You can visit Dora the Explorer any time at: www.nickjr.com. Dora is a Fisher-Price toy. Fisher Price inc. is a subsidiary of Mattel, Inc., New York. Dora is manufactured in China.

Cowgirl Dora (Value I)

Barney. Toysrus, Appleton Wisconsin. (Value I)

BARNEY

What child would not love this plush purple 14 inch Barney character, with his bright orange raincoat and rain cap? He is dressed for the rain, because he sings the song *If All the Raindrops.* Children will love singing along with Barney, "if all the raindrops were lemondrops and gumdrops..."

SPONGEBOB SQUAREPANTS

SpongeBob Squarepants is an animated talking doll measuring 5x5 inches. He requires three "AA" batteries to sing and talk. SpongeBob moves as he speaks. This yellow sponge is a cartoon hit with the children of 2003. He talks his SpongeBob language and sings: "Aye, Aye Captain, Argh, Argh, Argh!" He is made by the Mattel Company and manufactured in China. This toy can be purchased for under $8.00.

SpongeBob. (Value I)

Annabelle. Roxanne Wallis Collection. (Value I)

ANNABELLE BABY

Annabelle babbles, gurgles and giggles. Give her a bottle or pacifier and she sucks on it moving her mouth. After her meal she burps! A loud noise wakes her up and she cries. To calm Annabelle down, just talk, sing or shake her rattle. She will calm right down and babble happily again. Occasionally, after her bottle she has a tummy ache. Rub her tummy and she burps. She is almost as cute as a real baby. Baby Annabelle has a talking crib, baby walker and bouncy seat. She has The National Parenting Center Seal of Approval. Zapf Creation Inc. of Orlando, Florida is the creator of this lovable baby Annabelle. Her interior technical equipment is by Lernell Co. LLC and Mass Market Ideas LLC. Annabelle uses four "AA" batteries to become a real live baby.

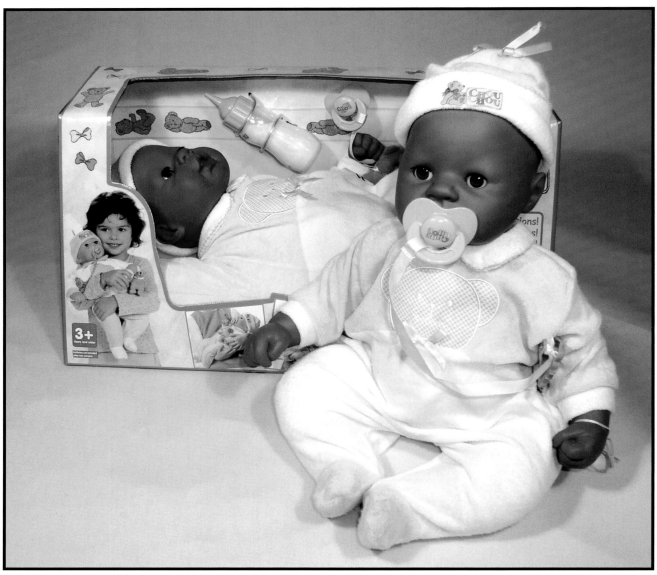

Rock A Bye Chou Chou. Roxanne Wallis Collection. (Value I)

ROCK A BYE CHOU CHOU BABY

Chou Chou laughs, cries and babbles like a real baby. Her lips move as she sucks her bottle. Lie her down and she yawns. Her eyes close when you rock her to sleep. If you pick her up when she is sleeping she will either wake up laughing or crying. Don't worry if she is crying, just pat her on the back and she will calm down. She comes with her bottle and pacifier. She is the perfect friend for children three years of age and older. Chou Chou can be purchased for $49.95. Her creator is Zapf Creation Inc.

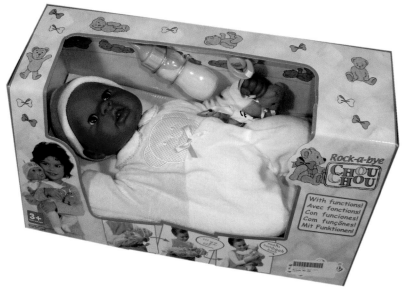

Baby CD Player. Toysrus, Appleton Wisconsin. (Value I)

BABY'S FIRST CD PLAYER

This CD player is for baby's crib, to soothe baby into slumber land. The CD player attaches securely to the crib rail and also has a night glow light. It comes with a CD titled *baby's bedtime classics* which features classics from Bach to Beethoven. Babies can now have their favorite CD selections anytime and grow to appreciate music from the day they are born. This 2003 CD player for baby is made by The First Years Inc., Avon, MA. It is manufactured in China.

DVD READ-ALONG

The magic of DVD technology has arrived. The concept of reading along with the new technology has not changed. Disney offers DVD's for children to read, sing and learn vocabulary words in five languages. Children can follow their favorite stories as they come to life, not from a book but from their television screen. They can sing along with their favorite Disney songs from *Toy Story, Monsters, Inc., Lilo & Stitch, The Little Mermaid,* and many more. The DVD offers hours of learning fun to educate and entertain children of the twenty-first century.

Disney Read-Along DVD. (Value I)

The Genius of Edison & Inventor Labs CD's. (Value I)

CD DISC

Harry Potter, The Hobbit, and *Winnie the Pooh* are now found on small compact discs that are read by a computer or CD player. Thomas Edison and other famous inventors are also found on the new media. *The Genius of Edison* is found on Compton's Home Library CD and the *InventorLabs* technology is a Houghton Mifflin interactive CD in which young inventors can explore the labs of Thomas Alva Edison, Alexander Graham Bell, and James Watt. These 5 inch compact discs are easy to use and "state of the art" in sound and picture quality.

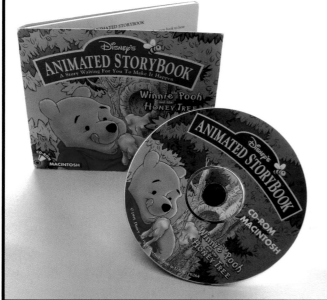

Winnie the Pooh CD. (Value I)

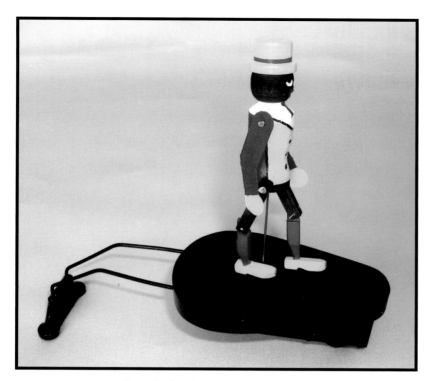

Reproduction Ragtime Rastus & Shimandy Dancers.   Charlie Weatherbee Collection. (Value H)

REPRODUCTION DANCING TOYS

It may be the computer age, but we are still fascinated by the hand crank phonographs and phonograph toys of yesteryear. We are even more fascinated by the phonograph dancing dolls that dance and wiggle when placed on the turntable. A collector and entrepreneur, Charlie Weatherbee, realized that these phonograph dancing dolls were still coveted by adults and children of all ages. Charlie made a series of phonograph dancing dolls that are quality hand crafted and purposely varied from the originals of the 1919 - 1920 era. The new series of phonograph dancing dolls are Ragtime Rastus, Boxing Darkies, Fighting Cocks, Shimandy and Banjo Billy. The ballroom Magnetic Dancers are also part of the series.

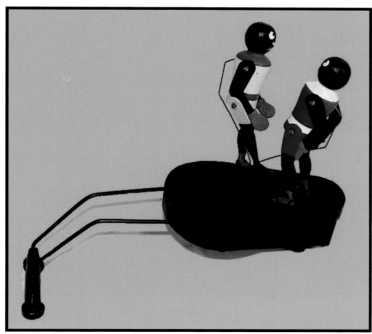

Reproduction Boxers. Charlie Weatherbee Collection. (Value H)

Rastus the terpsichorean artist is of wood construction and stands about 5 1/2 inches tall. He is handmade and painted the original colors of yellow, black, and red. The boxers are excellent reproductions of the real boxers of the 1900s era. They fight to the finish while the music is playing. Shimandy is of wood and steel spring construction about 6 1/2 inches tall. She is handmade and painted with a flowered patterned dress and felt hat. Her head tilts and rotates with her arms moving up and down when she dances. They dance on a platform that is nearly identical to the original. It mounts directly over the turntable spindle. The original platform needed the extra attachment ring and has the company name and patent dates imprinted on the underside of the platform.

Reproduction Banjo Billy. Charlie Weatherbee Collection. (Value H)

Reproduction Shimmy Sue.
John & Teri Andolina Collection. (Value G)

Banjo Billy, a reproduction phonograph dancing toy, was Charlie Weatherbee's own creation. Charlie used to play banjo when he had a Dixieland band in South Florida. All the original toys were black. Charlie had a very good friend named Bill and hence Banjo Billy was born. This imaginative performer is of wood construction and stands about 5 1/2 inches tall. He is handmade with a white face and painted in patriotic red, white, and blue. His right arm is loosely hinged and he appears to play his banjo while tap dancing.

Tuxedo Dancer & Edison Dancer.
Gfell Family Collection.

A Shimmy Sue was also made after the oriental fashion of Siam Soo. Shimmy Sue is made from a vintage puppet from India and dances the same Oriental dance as the original Siam Soo. The mechanism takes a considerable amount of work to re-create and produce. Shimmy Sue is only made by special order. The Magnetic Dancers and The Fighting Cocks are no longer being made. These reproduction dancers of 2000 are for the enjoyment and amusement of children of all ages. They are less expensive than the originals that command premium prices.

The concept of phonograph dancers is entertaining and fun. The Tuxedo Dancer and a dancer fashioned after the great inventor Thomas A. Edison were created by a craftsman, Greg Gfell, as a gift to his father, Don Gfell. To his father they are priceless. The dancing phonograph toys are an imaginative concept for entertainment and fun. We hope that collectors will enjoy both the vintage and reproduction dancers. Knowledge of the original and reproduction phonograph dancers is valuable to the customer when purchasing these phonograph toys that really gain your attention as they tap and dance their way into your heart and bring a smile to your face.

5-16

RCA DOLL & PUZZLES

The RCA doll, with her friends Nipper and Chipper, listening to her RCA radio with headphones, is typical of a computer age teen. This 18 inch doll is a cutie, dressed in her denim jeans and jacket, a pink tee shirt, tennis shoes and socks. This teenage doll of bisque porcelain does not talk, but represents the music loving kids of the year 2000.

Two RCA puzzles can still challenge children and their parents. A five hundred piece puzzle depicts the replica of the original stained glass window of Nipper and the Phonograph at the RCA Camden, N.J. landmark. In 1915, Eldridge Johnson, founder and president of the Victor Talking Machine Company had four stained glass windows, each measuring 14 1/2 feet in diameter, designed for the tower of the Victor Talking Machine Company's building #17D. They were placed in the tower in 1916. New Nipper stained glass windows were dedicated in 1978 and in 1987 the RCA Family Store offered this puzzling challenge to their customers.

In 1994 the EMI archives in England offered Nipper collectors a two hundred and fifty piece wooden jigsaw puzzle of the famous painting of Nipper looking into the phonograph. The painting by Francis Barraud is titled "His Master's Voice."

RCA Doll With Nipper & Chipper.   Joan Rolfs Collection.   (Value H)

"His Master's Voice" Stained Glass Window Puzzle.   (Value I)

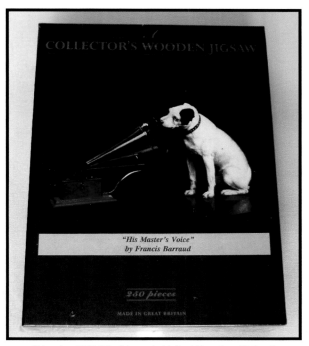

Wooden EMI "His Master's Voice" Puzzle.   (Value I)

THEODORE ROOSEVELT TALKING DOLL

Theodore Roosevelt recorded his historic speeches on Edison cylinders and Victor records. Toypresidents Inc., at www.toypresidents.com, released the Theodore Roosevelt talking figure in 2004. Produced as a limited edition of 10,000 this is a "doll" grownups will want to play with! Standing nearly 12 inches tall and wearing a "hand tailored" presidential suit, the doll contains a sound chip with 25 excerpts from Roosevelt's records for Edison and Victor.

Theodore Roosevelt Talking Doll. Steve Ramm Collection. (Value I)

One of the more popular speeches recorded by President Theodore Roosevelt on an Edison four minute wax cylinder is *The Farmer and Business Man.* An except from this cylinder can be heard at the push of the button. Lasting from 5 to 20 seconds, there are famous quotes as well as some short phrases from these historic recordings. The sound recordings are activated by pressing his lapel. The company currently has six Presidential figures to choose from and plans to produce others in the series. Each President is accompanied with a detailed biographical pamphlet including historic photographs and a timeline. This is a great way to teach kids about U.S. history.

Theodore Roosevelt Edison Amberol Recording.
Scott Malawski Collection. (Value G)

REPRODUCTION KAMMER AND REINHARDT TOY GRAMOPHONE

The early Kammer and Reinhardt toy gramophone has been reproduced by Ray Phillips of California. Ray is a highly regarded historian and collector in the phonograph community. The toy firm of Kammer and Reinhardt of Germany made the original toy from 1890 to 1894. The toy gramophone is authentically reproduced as a reproduction that collectors and children of the twenty first century can admire and enjoy.

Reproduction Kammer & Reinhardt Toy Phonograph.
John & Garnet Hauger Collection. (Value E)

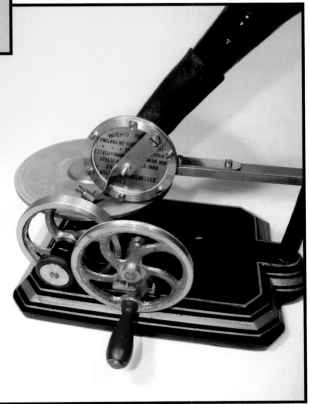

View of the Reproduction Mechanism of the Kammer & Reinhardt Toy Phonograph.

CONCLUSION

As we conclude this book, we read the reviews of the new digital dolls and toys. We find toy manufacturers today are facing the same challenges that Mr. Edison struggled with in 1890 when manufacturing his Edison Talking Doll. Today's materials and technology are vastly different than 115 years ago. Yet, the ambitions of producing and the goals of marketing products that will appeal to children as well as parents have not changed. With the development of soft plastics and solid state electronics that eliminate most moving parts, the dolls and toys of today should meet and exceed all expectations of both child and parent. Unfortunately science and engineering still underestimate the fortitude and determination of a child to find fault with a toy. The term "childproof" is not often taken seriously enough by the marketing analysts as the few pennies saved in production can be spent in packaging to entice product sales. Perhaps Mr. Edison after twelve years of frustration with "perfecting" the talking doll was the first to realize just how fragile a new technology can be in the hands of a child. What parent has never seen that look of disappointment, dismay and frustration overcome a child as a new toy breaks or malfunctions on Christmas morn? What parent has not experienced the anxiety as the toddler holds the pieces and pleads, "Please, fix this Daddy." At least Edison knew the best way out: Recall and dispose of the defective items in the New Jersey swamp and recoup losses with low-tech substitutes without talking mechanisms.

Some lessons are hard to learn as feedback from parents today echo sentiments similar to those in 1891. New technology has its tribulations. Comments like: "They really need to make children's toys with more durability---or at least price them accordingly." "The dresses on the princess were hard to remove; the interactive toys are always missing. We can hardly hear the doll talk, her voice is so faint." "The slightest brush against the CD player causes the CD to skip." "Be mindful that every time you turn the doll off, she must be reset--which can become a bit tedious." These reviews reflect similar comments made by children and parents of the late 1800s. What goes around comes around. Phonograph dolls are now digital dolls, children's records are now CD's and phonographs toys are now interactive toys. We can appreciate the early efforts and achievements by the inventors of phonograph dolls and toys. These dolls and toys taught, entertained, sang songs and most important brought smiles to children throughout time. Phonograph toys are the mirrors of life, reflecting in miniature the adult world.

Advertisement From the May 29, 1890 Issue of *Youth's Companion.* (Value I)

BIBLIOGRAPHY

ABFALTER, DOREEN: *Children's Records and Phonographs Presentation*
Michigan Antique Phonograph Society Phonovention 2000

AGNARD, JEAN-PAUL: *Making and Recording Edison Doll Wax Cylinders*
In The Groove, A Publication of MAPS 1998

AGNARD, JEAN-PAUL: *Phonograph Dolls*
Website http://www3.sympatico.ca/jean-paul.agnard/phonograph/collection.htm

ANDERTON, JOHANA GAST: *More Twentieth Century Dolls Volume Two I-Z*
Wallace Homestead Book Co. 1912 Grand Avenue, Des Moines, Iowa 1983

ANTON, JULIEN: *Le BeBe Jumeau Phonographe*
Coppelia, Bulletin De l'Association Des Amis Des Automates, Poupees et Juents Aciens.Paris France 1994

AUGUSTYNIAK, J. MICHAEL: *Thirty Years of Mattel Fashion Dolls, Identification & Value Guide 1957 through 1997*
Collector Books, Paducah, Kentucky 1998

AXE, JOHN A.: *Collector's Encyclopedia 1949 to Present*
Hobby House Press, Grandville, Maryland 1986

BEATO, ULISES: *Siam Soo She puts the O-O in Graf-on-ola*
Antique Phonograph Monthly, Vol IX - No. 1 Issue No. 81

BAUMBACH, ROBERT: *Look for the Dog An Illustrated Guide to Victor Talking Machines*
Mulholland Press Inc. Los Angeles, CA 90077 1981

BERLINER, OLIVER: *Nipper Happy 100th Birthday*
Beverly Hills, USA 1984

BILTON, LYNN: *Noteworthy News 2001 & Vintage Phonographs & Prices CD 2002*
Website: intertique.com

BROOKS, TIM: *Little Wonder Records A History and Discography*
The New Amberola Phonograph Co., 213 Caledonia Street, St. Johnsbury, VT 05819 1999

COLEMAN, DOROTHY S., ELIZABETH A, and EVELYN J.: *The Collector's Encyclopedia of Dolls*
Crown Publishers, Inc., New York 1968

CURRY, EDGAR L.: *VOGUE The Picture Record*
First Edition, Self-Published, Everett, Washington 1990

DARLING, ROBERT and CELIA with BRIAN RUST: *The Guiness Book of Recorded Sound*
Guiness Superlatives Ltd., Enfield, Middlesex 1984

ELLENBURG, KELLY M.: *EFFanBEE the Dolls with the Golden Hearts*
Trojan Press Inc. 310 E. 18th Ave., North Kansas City, Missouri 1973

FABRIZIO, TIMOTHY C. and PAUL, GEORGE F.: *The Talking Machine, an Illustrated Compendium 1877-1929*
Atglen (PA), Schiffer Publishing, Ltd., 1997

FABRIZIO, TIMOTHY C. and PAUL, GEORGE F.: *Antique Phonograph Gadgets, Gizmos & Gimmicks*
Atglen (PA), Schiffer Publishing, Ltd., 1999

FABRIZIO, TIMOTHY C. and PAUL, GEORGE F.: *Discovering Antique Phonographs 1877-1929*
Atglen (PA), Schiffer Publishing, Ltd., 2000

FABRIZIO, TIMOTHY C. and PAUL, GEORGE F.: *Phonographs with Flair: A Century of Style in Sound Reproduction*
Atglen (PA), Schiffer Publishing, Ltd., 2001

FABRIZIO, TIMOTHY C. and PAUL, GEORGE F.: *Antique Phonograph Accessories & Contraptions*
Atglen (PA), Schiffer Publishing, Ltd., 2003

FABRIZIO, TIMOTHY C. and PAUL, GEORGE F.: *Phonographica The Early History of Recorded Sound Observed*
Atglen (PA), Schiffer Publishing, Ltd., 2004

FEASTER, PATRICK: *The Sound of Life - The Prehistory of the Phonograph*
http://www.phonozoic.com

FITZGERALD, J.R.: *Siam Soo by J.R. Fitzgerald Website*
http://www.talkingmachine.org/siamsoo.html

FOULKE, JAN: *Blue Book of Dolls and Values*
Hobby House Press, Cumberland, Maryland.
Volume 4 1980, Volume 9 1989, Volume 11 1983, Volume 12 1995, Volume 13 1997

FROW, GEORGE L.: *Edison Cylinder Phonograph Companion*
Woodland Hills, Stationery X-Press, New York 1994

IZEN, JUDITH: *Collector's Guide to Ideal Dolls*
Collector' s Books, Paducah, Kentucky 1994

JOHL, JANET PAGTER: *Still More About Dolls,*
H.L. Lindquist Publications, New York, N.Y. 1950

JUDD, POLLY and PAM: *Hard Plastic Dolls--Identification*
Hobby House Press, Cumberland, Maryland 1985

KETTELKAMP, SEAN: *Chatty Cathy and Her Talking Friends*
Schiffer Publishing Company, Atglen, Pa. 1998

KURDYLA, JOHN PAUL JR.: *When Music Was Magic: History, Phonographs and Gramophones from 1879-1939*
Centrooffset, Mestrino, Padova, Italy 1987

KOENIGSBERG, ALLEN: The *Patent History of the Phonograph 1877-1912*
APM Press, Brooklyn, N.Y. 1990

KOENIGSBERG, ALLEN: *Turn-Table Toys of The Past*
Antique Phonograph Monthly, Vol. I, No. 4 1973

LEWIS, KATHY and DON: *Chatty Cathy Dolls*
Collector's Books, Paducah, Kentucky 1994

LEWIS, KATHY and DON: *Talking Toys of the 20th Century*
Collector's Books, Paducah, Kentucky 1999

LINDENBENGER, JAN and MORRIS, JUDY D.: *Encyclopedia of Cabbage Patch Kids of the 1980s*
Atglen (PA), Schiffer Publishing, Ltd., 1999

MALAWSKI, SCOTT: *The secret life of Siam Soo*
In The Groove, A Publication of MAPS 2003

MCFADDEN, SYBILL: *Mr. Edison's Astonishing Doll*
Hobbies Magazine, August 1983

MEHLING, JOHN: *Phonograph Doll Motor Cleaning and Lubricating*
In The Groove, A Publication of MAPS 1997

MAKEN, NEIL: *Hand-Cranked Phonographs - It all Started with Edison*
Yesterday Once Again, Huntington Beach, CA 1993

MARTY, DANIEL: *Illustrated History of Phonographs*
Dorset Press, New York 1981

MOYER, PATSY: *Doll Values, Antique and Modern*
Collector's Books, Paducah, Kentucky
First Edition 1997, Second Edition 1998, Third Edition 1999

MULDAVIN, PETER: *www.kiddierekordking.com*
173 W 78th St. NY, NY 10024. E-mail: Kiddie78s@aol.com

NAGLE, JOHN J.: *A Brief History of the National Company, Inc.*
AWA Review Volume I

PAUL, GEORGE: *The Johnson "Toy" Record The First Commercial 2-sided Disc*
The Antique Phonograph Monthly Vol. VIII No. 2

PETTS, LEONARD: *The Story of Nipper and the His Master's Voice Picture Painted by Francis Barraud*
1983 Talking Machine Review, 19 Glendale Road, Bournemouth, BH6 4JA, England

PHILLIPS, RAY: *Berliner's Gramophone - the Beginning*
For the Record, The Journal of the City of London Phonograph and Gramophone Society, No 3 - 2002

PILLE, STEPHAN: *Articles & Correspondence, Phonolist*
E-Group: phonolist@yahoogroups.com

POROT, ANN MARIE & JACQUES and FRANCOIS THEIMER: *S. F. B. J. Captivating Character Children*
Hobby House Press, Inc. Cumberland, Maryland 1986

ROLFS, JOAN: *The Phonograph Doll, She Sings, Recites & Walks*
In The Groove, A Publication of MAPS 1996

RONDEAU, RENE: *The Phonographs of Henri Lioret*
In The Groove, A Publication of MAPS 2002

RONDEAU, RENE: *"Mary Had a Little Fiasco" The Edison Talking Doll*
In The Groove, A Publication of MAPS 2003

SABULIS, CINDY: *Collector's Guide to Dolls of 1960s & 1970s*
Collector's Book, Paducah, Kentucky 2000

SCHENKER, W.: *The First German Gramophone Made By Emile Berliner*
The Hillandale News, No. 28, Dec. 1965, City of London Phonograph and Gramophone Society.

SEITER, BESSIE & FLOYD and ROLFS, JOAN & ROBIN: *Phonograph Dolls That Talk and Sing*
Audio Antique LLC W6273 Cedar Cliff Dr. Hortonville, WI 54944 2001

SIMONELLI, YOLANDA: *The Edison Talking Doll An Idea That Failed*
Doll Reader June/July 1988

SIMONELLI, YOLANDA: *The Madame Hendren and Mae Starr Phonograph Dolls*
Doll Reader October 1988.

SHERMAN, MICHAEL W.: *Collector's Guide to Victor Records*
Monarch Record Enterprise, Dallas, Texas 1992

SMITH, PATRICIA: *Doll Values, Antique and Modern*
Collector's Book, Paducah, Kentucky Ninth Edition 1993

SMITH, PATRICIA: *EFFanBEE Dolls That Touch Your Heart*
Collector's Book, Paducah, Kentucky 1983, updated 1998

SMITH, PATRICIA: *Modern Collector's Dolls*
Collector's Books, Paducah, Kentucky
Second Series 1975, Sixth Series 1994, Seventh Series1995, Eighth Series 1996

SPRINZEN, MERLE: *The Bubble Books*
In The Groove, A Publication of MAPS 2003

SUTTON, ALLAN and NAUCK, KURT: *American Record Labels and Companies An Encyclopedia (1891-1943)*
Mainspring Press, 9230 S. Buttonhill Ct./Highlands Ranch, CO 80126-4421 2000

TILLSON, DIANA R.: *The Golden Age of Children's Records*
Antique Phonograph News March-April 1995
Published by the Canadian Antique Phonograph Society

WEATHERBEE. CHARLIE: *Phonograph Dancing Dolls*
Hand Crank Phonographs-Charlie Weatherbee
2120 The Crescent
Clermont, FL 32711

WHITTON, MARGARET: *The Jumeau Doll*
Dover Publications Inc., New York 1980

WILKINS, JAMES R: *Olden Year Musical Museum*
131 West Fairmeadows, Duncanville, TX 75116

ZWERIN, MIRIAM: *A Talk with Noma*
Steelways Magazine, November 1951

INDEX

THE AUTHORS

Joan and Robin Rolfs have been collecting phonographs, phonograph dolls, phonograph toys, and phonograph memorabilia for the past thirty years. They have a love of preserving phonograph technology of the past for future generations. They co-authored a book with Bessie and Floyd Seiter in 2001 titled *Phonograph Dolls that Talk and Sing*. They have written articles relating to the phonograph hobby for *AntiqueWeek, The New Amberola Graphic, In The Groove, Fox Cities Magazine* and are editors of the *Badger Talking Machine*, a Wisconsin MAPS chapter newsletter. Their collection is also featured in the following books: *Discovering Antique Phonographs 1877-1929; Antique Phonograph Gadgets, Gizmos and Gimmicks; Antique Phonograph Accessories & Contraptions;* and *Antique Phonograph Advertising*.

Joan has a BS degree in Business/Interior Design. Robin has a BS and an MS degree in Technology Education. They are owners of Audio Antique LLC, a business that specializes in phonographs, dolls and related antiques from the Victorian period to the 1940's. Joan enjoys collecting phonograph dolls and Robin is enthralled by the technology of phonograph mechanisms. Together they make a great team to present and share exciting new information in the area of phonograph dolls, toys and records for children. The authors can be contacted at www.audioantique.com

French Plate, Circa 1900s. Julian Anton Collection. (Value F)